CW01476451

PE]

war

David Slack is a speechwriter, commentator and author of *Bullshit, Backlash & Bleeding Hearts*. A graduate in law from Victoria University of Wellington, he has worked as a speechwriter in the Prime Minister's office. He is associated with a variety of Internet websites including *www.speeches.com*, *www.PublicAddress.Net*, and a companion site for this publication, *www.optimisticpredictions.com*. He lives in Devonport with his wife and daughter.

David Slack

CIVIL WAR

{... & Other optimistic predictions}

where is new zealand going?

PENGUIN BOOKS

PENGUIN BOOKS
Published by the Penguin Group
Penguin Group (NZ), cnr Airborne and Rosedale Roads, Albany,
Auckland 1310, New Zealand
Penguin Books Ltd, 80 Strand, London, WC2R 0RL, England
Penguin Group (USA) Inc., 375 Hudson Street, New York, NY 10014, United States
Penguin Group (Australia), 250 Camberwell Road, Camberwell,
Victoria 3124, Australia
Penguin Books Canada Ltd, 10 Alcorn Avenue, Toronto,
Ontario, Canada M4V 3B2
Penguin Books (South Africa) (Pty) Ltd, 24 Sturdee Avenue, Rosebank,
Johannesburg 2196, South Africa
Penguin Books India (P) Ltd, 11, Community Centre, Panchsheel Park,
New Delhi 110 017, India
Penguin Ireland Ltd, 25 St Stephen's Green, Dublin 2, Ireland
Penguin Books Ltd, Registered Offices: 80 Strand, London, WC2R 0RL, England

First published by Penguin Group (NZ), 2005
1 3 5 7 9 10 8 6 4 2

Copyright © David Slack, 2005

The right of David Slack to be identified as the author of this work in terms of
section 96 of the Copyright Act 1994 is hereby asserted.

Designed by Mary Egan
Typeset by Egan Reid Ltd
Printed in Australia by McPherson's Printing Group

ISBN 0 14 301994 5
A catalogue record for this book is available
from the National Library of New Zealand.

www.penguin.co.nz

Contents

For Karren

Preface

THIS IS a book that was first conceived as the second edition to another. As I was completing *Bullshit, Backlash & Bleeding Hearts* in 2004, the political issues it described were evolving swiftly. The hikoi marched on Parliament, the Foreshore and Seabed legislation was passed, Tariana Turia left the government and emerged as a leader of the Maori Party. A reprint of the book was looming, and we discussed a second edition to incorporate developments, and perhaps broaden its scope. That book, though, had been written as an accessible summary of a complex topic. Broadening and deepening it would possibly be counter-productive. Instead, it seemed preferable to incorporate that additional material in a new book, paying particular attention to recent political debate. Given that aspects of the debate had included some dire predictions about the nation's future, the question seemed obvious: why not explore the gloomy thread that runs through New Zealand life? Why not take a few of the most doom-laden warnings, and haul them out into the light?

I am obliged to the many people who made themselves available to share their thoughts on these topics. Many of them, it will be clear from the text, are neither gloomy nor unduly anxious about our nation's future. Nevertheless, some are at least a little perturbed, and have some concerns that merit careful thought. Many will be familiar to readers, but for completeness' sake, are introduced here.

A variety of politicians are quoted. Deborah Coddington is a former journalist and ACT member of Parliament. Jeanette Fitzsimons is the co-leader of the Green Party. Stephen Franks is the ACT party justice spokesperson. Although his province is more ecclesiastic than political, it is perhaps not inaccurate to include Brian Tamaki, the leader of the Destiny Church in this category also.

A variety of people provided a helpful business and economic perspective: Roger Kerr, who is the executive director of the New Zealand Business Roundtable; Tim Hazledine, Professor of Economics at Auckland University; Wayne Hope who is a senior lecturer in media studies at AUT, and Rod Oram who is a financial commentator and journalist.

On matters relating to Treaty issues and the relationship between Maori and Pakeha, a number of authorities are quoted, and I am grateful to them all for their contributions. Margaret Mutu is Professor of Maori Studies at Auckland University; Andrew Sharp is Professor in Political Studies at Auckland University; Hekia Parata's career has included roles in Foreign Affairs and Te Puni Kokiri, and on the boards of New Zealand On Air and the Ngai Tahu Development Corporation. Chris Trotter is a writer and commentator, and a proprietor and editor of the *NZ Political Review*. 'Esteemed historian and academic' is perhaps the most concise description of Bill Oliver, whose accomplishments, to name just two, include his authorship of *Oxford History of New Zealand* and the *Dictionary of New Zealand Biography*.

I am particularly grateful to Russell Brown, not only for sharing his thoughts on the grave problems facing the nation in the form of 'political correctness' and 'social engineering', but also because it was he who encouraged me to take some time away from my speech writing work to contribute to his

PublicAddress.net blog site. That in turn has led to a variety of assignments in commentary and writing which have all been as fulfilling as they have been enjoyable.

I also thank *Reality* magazine for permission to reprint their story of Linda Papuni's experience of life through Maori and Pakeha eyes.

I especially want to thank the good people at Penguin New Zealand – notably Finlay Macdonald and Alison Brook – for shepherding this book through the process of publication, and providing the author with much-appreciated insight and encouragement.

Finally and most importantly, I want to thank my wife Karren and daughter Mary-Margaret for their forbearance over the intrusion of this project into our Christmas holidays. Our interrupted summer turned out to be far better than any of the predictions, and – in the end – one of the best in years. There is, perhaps, a small lesson in that.

Introduction

THE ONLY certainties in horse racing, as the old saying goes, are bills and disappointment. Dad's family loved horses – rode them, bred them, raced them. I grew up to the sound of the first and second leg of the double from Ellerslie and a full call of the card from Awapuni. Punting wasn't the most interesting aspect to me, not at first. But that changed the day I picked a winner in the first race at Wanganui paying ninety-three dollars for the win. (One of the Lupton family's horses, racing in the colours that Kiwi made famous, if you follow these things.) That set me up for a decade or so of gambling until I came to realise it was more of a low-paid weekend job than a diversion. There were, surely, smarter ways to get lucky.

It took me longer than most. Much of the nation had already fallen out of whatever love it had for horse racing. My old friend Jack Glengarry, the only racing writer to jog around every single racecourse in the country, would be able to tell you how many of them are closed now. New Zealanders are still gamblers, though: at the pokie machines, at the housie, at the casinos and at the Lotto outlets.

But do we feel lucky? Well, do we? The neighbours do, or at least they profess to. The 'lucky country' started from pretty unpromising beginnings, and yet look at them now: proud, confident, loaded with minerals, and anointing a new 'Great Australian' every other moment. If it weren't for the not-by-any-means-convenient matter of running out of water at some point in the future – ten years for Perth, evidently – you'd say they had it made. And even though the rollercoaster has swooped them up and down most of the same peaks and gullies as us – gold-rush boom and bust, influenza epidemic at the end of the Great War, long unemployment lines in the Depression, mad Labour Party socialists enfeebling the nation with a welfare state, Japanese bombing Darwin, wool price slump – not to mention the moment in history that seems to gather in significance with every anniversary: Gallipoli – they really don't seem to have shared our outlook. Through all the defeats and disasters – all the same things that were going to send us to the wall – there doesn't seem, in their history, to be the same thread of brooding and foreboding that runs through ours.

When you add it all up, they don't have it bad: the minerals in the ground, the fertile land, the glorious climate, and the liberated spirit that perhaps only a society founded by transported convicts can feel. Maybe the correct label *is* lucky. But line their list up against ours. We're not *that* different. So why do we have this heritage of regarding our existence here as a gamble that could send us broke *any hand now*? The Australians act as though they don't expect to draw anything less than a full house, and they'll do it *any night you like, pal.*

This is a book about our future here in New Zealand, and how we rate the odds of our gamble. If, in fact, it is a gamble. It's not so much an inquiry into why Australia is a *glass-half-full* sort of nation while we tend more to the *glass-is-half-empty-and-the-tonic's-flat* point of view, so much as it's a demonstration that some of the issues we're most gloomy or extreme about are not nearly so dire as some people make them out to be.

I've been hearing gloom and doom in this country for as long as I can remember, and yet somehow the dark fate waiting just around the corner has never quite managed to get its clammy hands on us. So what went right, so many times? How did we manage to get rescued from the railroad tracks in the nick of time with such regular good fortune? Or could it be that we weren't in quite such a jam in the first place?

Lately we've been hearing from a variety of concerned New Zealanders about some terrible problems and some quite dire consequences that lie just around the corner if we don't do something about them. Don Brash, for one. He famously warned the nation at the beginning of 2004 that we were on a dangerous drift to separatism. Later that year, he worried in the *Australian Financial Review* that New Zealand risked becoming 'just another Pacific Island state'. He has not been alone. Doomsayers have predicted everything from the collapse of decent values to civil war.

I'm not suggesting that we're a nation of gloom merchants standing hunched shoulder to hunched shoulder and looking darkly inwards. The place is full of people willing to try something new. Overrun with them, in fact. But we also have a choir droning steadily and tunelessly in the background to let us know that *it will never work* and pointing out the ten ways it will go wrong. The approved way to sing along to this non-tune is to take a long slow intake of breath through pursed lips, accompanied by a slowly shaking head and an expression that is one part sneer and two parts triumphant smirk.

Even though these people may sometimes be right, they deserve altogether less attention. The other side to that particular coin deserves some attention too, and that's the mindlessly positive cheerleading that borders on zealotry. At moments in our recent history – the KZ7 months that preceded the stock market crash come to mind – we have seemed capable of lurching from one extreme to the other in just days. If a country were capable of psychoanalysis, my bet for us would be: manic depressive.

It's not that we don't have some capability for accommodating multiple cultures and handling diversity; we do. But for everyone who's *up for it*, we have a dozen people who can't be bothered breaking out of their fixed point of view about the way they want New Zealand to be. I want to explore the possibilities for tolerance, for plurality, and for adaptation.

It's not that we don't have prospects for lifting our standard of living and solving some of our old social problems; we do. But for all that we know about making it happen, we have a gallery of critics who will tell you why it won't work. I want to explore some of our opportunities for building on what we have.

And it's not that we're not capable of adapting and developing our attitudes; we are. But there's a strong thread of bigotry and small-mindedness and selfishness that gets plenty of rein here. It deserves to be outed.

What follows is an exploration of the coming apocalypse, in three parts: we'll look first at War, then Famine and finally Plague & Pestilence. At the risk of spoiling the ending, let me say now that I confidently predict that we will manage to dodge them all. Except maybe the Plague.

Maybe I should emphasise this: I do not believe we will have civil war and I do not advocate it. But the topic came up last year, and it didn't come up for no reason at all. I think it's sensible that we ask why it emerged, and see where that takes us. I also believe that we have a perfectly good prospect of steering our economy through another hundred years without necessarily seeing it dropping through the floor, and I believe that the various plagues and pestilences of political correctness, social engineering, and tolerance for diversity are unlikely to impel us headlong towards Hell in any form of cart or basket.

All of this is not to say that nations can't and don't fail, but a head cold is not a terminal illness. As gambles go, New Zealand strikes me as one of the safer ones. Having said that, we have to accept a few qualifications to the proposition. A meteor of dinosaur-extinguishing quality could severely disrupt Business Confidence here in New Zealand, and that is always a Very Bad Thing. Likewise foot-and-mouth disease, likewise some kind of Asian bird flu pandemic. Also, see: Wellington earthquake 2015, Indonesian invasion 2025, and World Oil War 2027. But all of those could equally apply to Australia, and you don't see them putting away their money. The resources you're favoured with have a lot less to do with your prosperity than what your people do with their skills. You can do that sitting on little more than a rock, as Singapore and Hong Kong have demonstrated.

So, we're on a safe bet then? Pretty safe, in my opinion. But because you can never say these things with absolute confidence, we'll spend the next couple of hundred pages assessing the odds anyway. And just to make it interesting, as the old song goes, we'll have a shilling on the side. You'll find a reference at the end of each of the three sections to a companion website. At www.optimisticpredictions.com you'll be able to register for $1500 of gambling money (actual value: nil) which you can use to wager on the likelihood of the various dire predictions touted in the book coming to pass. This is an experiment, drawing on the wisdom of the markets. It's a practice long-enough established in commodities markets, where you speculate on the future price of everything from crude oil to pork bellies. In recent times, you've seen the same thing happening to less mercantile pursuits – the presidency of the United States for example. The money has turned out to be pretty accurate. Crass? Absolutely. Irresponsible? Possibly. And for that reason, it doesn't let you bet on the odds of a civil war. Some things aren't to be taken frivolously. Also, there's a chap already up on a sedition charge for writing leaflets about Treaty-related unrest. Apart from that, though, the house is accepting all comers. Life's a gamble and we're a long time dead; so, ladies and gentlemen, place your bets.

War

Chapter One

6 February 2040

The White House, Washington DC

President Chelsea Clinton expressed cautious optimism for New Zealand's future at the signing this afternoon of an historic peace agreement between the oil-rich South Pacific nation's Interim Authority and the insurgent Maori Liberation Movement.

Earlier peace negotiation efforts by Clinton's predecessor Barack Obama had yielded only brief ceasefire intervals in the long-running conflict, and observers are sceptical about the prospects for this latest initiative.

The uprising has its origins in the so-called 'In-by-lunchtime' deployment of US Marines in the summer of 2011 when President Jeb Bush, acting on the invitation of incoming New Zealand Prime Minister Gerry Brownlee, sent in Marines to disperse Maori protestors barricading the vast Watson-Hart oilfield off the coast of the country's hydrocarbon-rich Taranaki region.

'The world has hoped for many years now that New Zealanders might set aside their differences and bring an end to the bloodshed,' the President said. 'Let us hope that day has finally come.'

Shares in Halliburton-Telecom closed slightly higher on the news, and crude oil eased to 300 Yuan a barrel.

PREDICTING the future is a tricky business. It can make fools of the smartest of people. But that's not to say that we don't have some intuitive sense of the likelihood of things. If your intuition's anything like mine, you'll say that we have a pretty good instinct for steering ourselves away from trouble before things get out of hand. Your typical New Zealander would probably say that civil war in a place like Auckland or Gisborne was a ridiculous idea and – more to the point – that anyone who would suggest it would have to be some kind of idiot or at least a bit of a shit-stirrer.

It might be wise to pause for a moment and consider the assumption I've just made: what does the 'typical New Zealander' look like, exactly? Can we read his or her mind? I quite like the argument that takes people to task for speaking on behalf of 'the silent majority': if they're silent, how do you know how many of them there are? Wouldn't it be more accurate to call them the silent people? And given that they're not talking, how can you know what they're thinking? All in all, the best description you can give them is: 'my imaginary friends'. So: without some evidence to support what I've just claimed, I have to admit that it's simply a sense I have; I don't know it for certain. A better place to begin might be to put the burning question to someone who has actually predicted such a calamity: what were you thinking?

The year 2004 was a big one for the politics of division in New Zealand. The leader of the Opposition fretted about the dangers of preferential treatment for Maori, while many Maori fretted about the treatment they were getting from the leader of the Opposition. And as if that weren't enough, the Government pushed ahead with legislation regarding the ownership of the foreshore and seabed of the country that appeared to many Maori – those of them who joined a 20,000-strong hikoi to Parliament at least – to look more like land grab than leadership.

Debate raged, and along the way an unwelcome tone found its way into the national conversation: *it could come to civil war.* Imagine for a moment you're a journalist. It comes to your attention that amongst the 4000-odd submissions to the Select Committee holding hearings on the Foreshore and Seabed Bill, there's one by a senior public servant which makes this warning: *This country could be brought to its knees by internal conflict and perhaps civil war over the coming decades as a direct result of this bill.* Do you have a story? The *Sunday Star-Times* certainly thought so. At the beginning of August that year, they reported that Maori Language Commission chief executive Haami Piripi, had written just such a submission. In hindsight, they reported, he conceded that he would have toned down his language. But he would still have made the submission: 'I was about as angry as I get.' He said he had used those terms to express the strength of his convictions. 'This law is going to bring trouble . . .'

Condemnation came quickly, and in large measure. Politicians wanted his resignation, or at least an apology. Piripi, for his part, was resolute. As the disciplinary steps ensued, he apologised for the tone but not the substance of his comments and defended his right to speak as a concerned citizen about legislation that had the potential 'to blow this country apart'. And later that month, Professor Margaret Mutu, who is head of Maori Studies at Auckland University, endorsed his argument before the same select committee. And like Piripi, she points out, she was speaking not as a public servant, but on behalf of her people in Karikari, the *Ngati Kahu*:

As soon as this thing hit the fan, twenty-third of June 2003, Margaret Wilson announces that she's going to confiscate our foreshore and seabed. Now, Ngati Kahu met after that, I mean the anger was raw, absolutely raw.

Ngati Kahu, she explains, were already feeling frustrated about the harm that was being done to the coastline: 'You've got several billionaire Americans buying there and establishing settlements, developments really, and then not having the proper infrastructure to deal with it.' Sewage, she says, is a big problem: 'It's wrecking all of our marine environments.'

We had been fighting that for ten, fifteen years, and we had got so fed up with not being able to do anything that we had actually issued public notices saying that *nothing happens around our coast any more without our permission*. Because the people who are supposed to be managing this area are stuffing it up something wicked. And I mean this is a relatively low population area, we are trying to stop the impacts of more and more coming in.

The Foreshore and Seabed issue, it seemed to Ngati Kahu, stood to weaken their position very substantially. They worried about their capacity to protect the waters around them. What control could they exert if they were seen to have no title? By June of 2003, some kaumatua in their seventies were getting especially staunch.

They just said: *If we have to go to war, we go to war. And what's wrong with you people? When your land gets taken off you, if you've got to hold on to it by force, you hold on to it by force* . . . and a lot of them − even in that hui − were saying: *Be careful. Be careful about that sort of talk*. But the anger was so high that these other ones kept saying: *How much more are you going to have to have taken off you before you are going to stand up and say 'No bloody more!' and actually do it?*

So there was a raw anger . . . and I'd say *Right, now I'm going off down to the hui at Hauraki. What am I to say when I go down there?*

And the instructions were: *You tell them there's no bloody way . . .* And we had meetings after that, and every time it's always: *Right, now Margaret's going to so and so, what's she going to say?* Because I said: *You people, you're going to send me up there to do this, but by crikey you'd better make sure that what I say is right.* And so in that first period they said to me: *Don't talk about war.*

Okay, I said, *fine.* And so you'll find that I haven't mentioned anything about it. And then you had the debacle over Haami Piripi, when Haami said it. Now Haami is one of ours. And they were furious. Absolutely furious that somebody who's a civil servant and very, very conservative – he's not out there doing anything radical – says something to warn the government and they treat him like they did. And they just said to me: *No, you've got to defend our relation.*

So. That's why when I went to the select committee I said: *When a senior civil servant warns you of what this is, and how bad this thing is that you are going to visit on the country, you would be extremely unwise not to listen to him.*

And then, of course, in the actual select committee hearing itself, [National's] Wayne Mapp was saying to me: *How dare you mention the words civil war?* He gave me a big lecture about being a professor at university and he said: *Well, what do you mean by civil war?* And I said: *For heaven's sake, everybody knows what a civil war is.* And he said: *No, no, no, exactly what is a civil war?* I said: *Well you've got heaps of them going on in the world at the moment.*

Well, he said, *what is it?* I said: *Well what you've got going on in Palestine at the moment is a civil war.* And then they drew all sorts of other things from it that really had nothing to do with the fact that I was saying: *For God's sake listen. Listen to what you're being told. Because this thing* – what I was trying to gently say to them is: *The raw anger you've got out there in the communities, is very, very raw.*

And that, says Margaret Mutu, is when people started asking her how such a thing would happen. She described a possible sequence of events: 'Somebody turns up in front of my house and decides to set up a marine farm without my permission. I will go down very politely and ask them to please move themselves, and they will say: *Well I have a legal right to be here*, and I'll say: *No you don't have a legal right to be here.*'

Then, she says, she will go away and it will be her nephews – the ones who are angry – who will go down and demolish it. 'And they say: *Oh well, we will just send the police*, and I said: *No, you'll have to send the army in. Because it won't be just one group, behind them will be a whole lot more. And a whole lot more.*'

Solidarity amongst iwi, she says, was strong. Ngati Kahu were dealing with a case in the Mangonui Harbour and asked other iwi if they had their support. If the authorities should refuse to listen to them – as mana whenua – about the matter, would the other iwi come in behind them? Yes, they said, they would come.

> And then they said: *Well, Te Rarawa's dealing with something over at Whangape, if that all goes to custard will you come and help us over there?* We said: *Of course we will.* And so when Te Rarawa called for that hands-across-the-beach thing on Ninety Mile Beach [protesting against the Seabed and Foreshore legislation], we all went in to help. Now that was a message to the Crown. Every iwi up there came together to support Te Rarawa, because Te Rarawa asked for the support. And we did. We all turned up.
>
> Now that's a very symbolic Maori way of doing things. It was a show of strength which said: *You threaten us and this is what we will do. We'll call in our troops. But our troops will have children and old people in them as well. And we will dare you to do anything to us when the children, the adults, the old people are all there on the beach trying to protect what is theirs – are you going to kill them?*
>
> And that's the message that they were sending out, that we would do this as peaceably as we could, but we weren't going to shift on it. And I know that some of those younger ones, if I was to step back, I'd just let them go and then . . .

The risk, then, lies in dismissing the concerns of an aggrieved minority? 'I can see it happening if there is this blindness, and that's why I'd always hoped that there was this reasonableness and this fairness . . . that would temper it.'

The Government, of course, would say that it could not have tried harder to listen to the concerns of Maori. It wasn't possible to build a full consensus on the issue but they could not do *nothing*, they said – because that would leave uncertainty hanging over a contentious issue. Deputy Prime Minister Michael Cullen, in an interview with the *New Zealand Herald*, asked what the Government was supposed to do – accept the argument that Maori owned the foreshore and seabed . . . 'or do we reinforce the current law which actually does say the Crown owns the foreshore and seabed?' He argued that the Government was resolving the unresolvable by creating some recognition of customary rights.

But is there such a thing as a compromise that will work? Margaret Mutu points out that this is a clash between two very different ways of viewing your relationship with the land: one is the English notion, which has a very strong ownership aspect to it.

> When the Crown grants title, it guarantees that person has undisturbed possession of that land and has the right to sell it or lease it. Or whatever they wish to do – alienate it or whatever they want. Now that's a very English notion. And what we are asking for is recognition of a Maori notion that is really quite different from that.
>
> The Maori notion is much more about the rights that you have – having been there for many, many generations (in many cases that's many, many hundreds of years) – as something that was given to you originally by the gods. And you have a responsibility to maintain that area intact for the following generations. So the notion of you having something that you

control as a commodity is just not there. At all.

. . . you are very much a part of where you are. So you will often hear Maori say: *You desecrate my river or my sea, you desecrate me.* Because you're part of it. It's a very, very different notion from the notion of ownership. But the notion of ownership is that you will have undisturbed possession, you will have control, you will have authority, and that sort of thing. *That* is part of mana whenua. It's just alienation that is not.

Mutu mentions a comment that fellow academic Ranginui Walker once made, that the British came in as if sovereignty had been ceded and Maori carried on as if sovereignty had not been ceded and the two just were different lives.

And I have to say in the Far North . . . we do still live two separate lives and . . . when I go up there, I live according to tikanga [Maori laws and practices]. And it's just natural, it's just the way things are. I am aware that the neighbours down the road from me live according to another set of rules. When they try to come onto my land, I will always say to them: *You come in here on my conditions.* And it works in the rural areas because we are not in each other's faces all the time and there's distance. It works well.

So. The government might very well say that they were enacting something more palatable than a bald declaration that the land did not belong to Maori, but if your people have been arguing for a century and a half that the land has never actually been alienated in the sense that the Crown understands it, you're going to have a problem.

This may not sit easily with the *one-law-for-all New Zealanders* point of view, and we'll explore the issue in coming chapters. But putting larger principles aside for a moment, let's consider this: the fact that people with these quite different perspectives on ownership can be living alongside one another and going about their daily lives without clashing begs a question: How much will it matter in everyday life that the law now says something about ownership of the foreshore and seabed that is not accepted by its opponents? From time to time, push may well come to shove, as Margaret Mutu suggests, but if other examples of Maori protest by occupation are any guide, it's hard to imagine there won't still be room for calm heads to negotiate. What she describes looks more like a defensive posture than an aggressive one.

Of course, we've only been only considering one specific issue. Aside from the foreshore and seabed, could there be other minefields to consider? The hikoi was, the organisers said, a march on Parliament to object to the confiscation of land under the Foreshore and Seabed legislation, but you only had to hear a few interviews with the protestors to get the clear sense that people had a range of reasons for marching.

Writer and commentator Chris Trotter would probably concede that he has not been an especially optimistic voice in the debate over race and Treaty matters. Given the expression of discontent by Maori, how does he rate the chances for an incoming National government of implementing their *one law for all*: 'I don't think it's possible.' He says that although it makes him fearful for the near future of the country, he sees it as 'a kind of historical necessity' that there should be some sort of clash between Maori and Pakeha. Why? Because people won't otherwise have the will to address the renewal of the covenant – 'if you want to use that loaded expression' – that was made between Maori and Pakeha in 1840. He argues that a new covenant 'definitely needs to be made between the two peoples' because the Treaty wasn't between Maori and Pakeha; the Treaty was between Maori chiefs and 'the super-chief, the uber-chief in London. It is an aristocratic pact. It is not a democratic document. And what needs to be thrashed out is the relationship between the people who have been here for 600 or 700 years and the people who have been here for one or two. That's what needs to be thrashed out, and it won't happen until there's a clash'.

What kind of clash does he contemplate? 'A big event. A Springbok tour. I hope not a bomb going off somewhere. Or gunfire erupting somewhere. I really hope it doesn't come to that. I hope it's much more a '51 or an '81.' He says it's hard to be more certain because 'the times we live in produce such bizarre behaviour in people'.

> But I think there is something in Pakeha and Maori which makes them step back at the last. You recognise something in each other that is necessary to us and I think you saw that in the way Pakeha reacted to the hikoi. And [Paul] Holmes' comment . . . he said on the day of the hikoi: 'No New Zealander frankly could have watched proceedings today without a sense of pride, without being gripped by the heart, could have watched it without love.' Because we recognised something there. I think Pakeha of goodwill saw the expression of Maori hurt at Orewa, not just the foreshore and seabed. But I think they saw the hurt and they saw the pride in themselves and [said] *You can't do it, Don! You can say how angry we are but you can't do it!* What's he going to do if a Maori party wins all the Maori seats. Is he going to abolish them?

Could a fallback position for National then be to convene some grand convention upon the topic? Trotter says that's always been the Right's most sensible course of action, 'but then the Right have been conservative chaps, they haven't grasped that'.

> But it was always there for ACT and National to set themselves up as the constitutional parties. The ones that would actually take the radical steps and let the chips fall where they may. But they haven't done that.

He believes it's theoretically possible for the Crown to do another Bastion Point, although he wonders whether the New Zealand State has the power, '*the sheer force*', at its disposal. The New Zealand Navy, he points out, which has traditionally been the force designated to come to the aid of the civil power – 'as it nearly did up here in Auckland the last day of the Springbok tour' – is now completely bicultural. It devotes great attention to Maori protocol and tradition, and has a great many Maori in its ranks. 'If it came to mass demonstrations and protest, things getting out of control, I just wonder whether if some Pakeha gave the order, Maori ratings would fire.' The Army, he points out, has an even greater proportion of Maori, and the SAS more still.

> See, I'm just not sure whether if a politician gave the order, whether in fact it would be carried out. That's something I think our politicians might like to ponder long and hard. Because in the end, the State is the body which commands the monopoly on violence, and if you cease to control that monopoly then you cease to be a state, that's the way it plays.

Historian Bill Oliver is not so sure about that. Army people he meets are more conservative than anyone he's come across: 'That may not be the rank and file, but the officer class certainly are – the entire inheritance of Sandhurst and all the rest.' We do forget, he points out, how many Maori fought with the British in the 1860s.

But back to the present: would there actually ever come a day when they were asked to fire? New Zealanders, Chris Trotter suggests, have a tendency to pat themselves on the back for their pragmatic and even-headed ways of resolving problems: 'The number of times I've heard people saying: *Oh Chris, this isn't Bosnia, you know. It's not Northern Ireland, it's not Palestine, these sorts of things wouldn't happen in New Zealand.* But I just invite people to imagine what would have happened in 1981 if someone had been killed. On either side.' The potential, he argues, was always there for a spiral of violence to begin: first you get the retribution, then the counter-attack, then the counter-counter-attack and very quickly you're pitched into something quite disastrous.

New Zealanders, he recalls, 'really surprised themselves' in the upheaval of the 1981 Springbok tour at how passionate they could get about issues. He was, he says, 'staggered at how quickly you learn to identify your social enemy'.

> And it came very close. I got death threats as the editor of the student newspaper. My wife's house was surrounded by people who threatened to kill her. Hamilton in 1981 the day that the game was called off – I remember dear old Wolfgang Rosenberg said that it reminded him of Kristallnacht. He came from Austria in the thirties and, he said, exactly the same feeling. There were people out there who would kill you if they could find you because of what you believed. We were lucky. We were lucky in '51 during the waterfront dispute. I think there were some industrial accidents there of people called in to do work which was dangerous and which they weren't trained to do, but there wasn't a fusillade of police fire knocking down 20 or 30 people, as there could so easily have been if things had been just that little bit more . . .

He thinks the Queen Street riots in the Depression could have gone the other way too, if it hadn't been for the fact that it took the authorities a reasonable amount of time to bring the situation under control. 'The next night the mounted specials from Waikato were up in K Road. They charged into people there.' He also points back to the gun battle of Taranaki Street during the general strike in 1913.

> Once again, just sheer dumb luck. Both sides, having at each other. Bullets flying in the darkness. Police firing, strikers firing.

No one was killed. Because the bullets just kept on missing –
and they kept on missing right through our history, and it's
remarkable.

But was it entirely dumb luck? Could it be that there is a realism
that takes hold when the stakes get too high? For example, what
might happen if a National Party-led administration of some
kind were to take power and deliver a truly robust platform of
assimilation: 'one law for all'; no 'special treatment' for Maori;
a wholesale dismantling of bicultural policies? Trotter thinks it
would strike more trouble than it could handle. He suggests
there are a number of people – 'even in the National Party' –
who realise that the hikoi demonstrated that you couldn't
contemplate implementing an assimilationist agenda without
using 'massive repression'.

> Sid Holland wanted to break the back of the left-wing unions
> but he had to bring in the emergency regulations in 1951 to do
> it. And he had to have 151 days of essentially fascist government
> to bring it about.

Unless Don Brash was prepared to do something like that, he
says, he would have a very big challenge. There were only
20,000 people involved in the trade union federation in 1951,
he points out. There are perhaps 250,000 who identify themselves primarily as Maori, and repressing that many people, he
argues, 'is a very different kettle of fish to repressing 20,000'.

> I am fearful of what might happen. I watched that hikoi and I
> saw Hone Harewera controlling that body with the skill of a
> Maori battalion commander and it was peaceful, but I looked
> at him and I saw that a man who can keep 20,000 people
> peaceful could probably just as easily have them not be peaceful,
> and if Brash missed the message, he was very, very foolish.
>   I was very impressed by Hone's control. I have met him
> subsequently and he's a very impressive man, a warrior. Reborn.

From the past. Maori warriors are not to be trifled with, it seems to me.

If your name is Don Brash and you're wondering at this page of the book whether you can be bothered reading any further, Bill Oliver offers a slightly more hopeful view:

> My guess is that most New Zealanders whatever their group and including Maori as a whole have not actually given up hope of getting somewhere. And I would also guess that the readiness of Pakeha society to go some distance to meet Maori demands ... for whatever multitude of reasons... not altogether the same, goes a long way to account for that.

However, he also admits some concerns. He recalls hearing a lecture at Auckland University by the historian Alan Ward towards the end of the 1990s. 'At the end a young guy stood up and said: *Look, can you give me any good reason why I should not start – or me and my friends start – buying AK-47s?*' Ward, he says, was – not surprisingly – taken aback.

> The answer which Alan and I worked out later on is to say: *Yes, there is one pretty good reason. The first is that you would be killed and what's worse is that a lot of people more innocent than you would be killed with you . . .*

How far, he wonders, can Maori push before a Pakeha majority might shove back? Suppose your more vocal figures in the debate were to take a strong position – Margaret Mutu, Pita Sharples, Moana Jackson and Pakeha like Jane Kelsey, for example. He believes there's a risk that can come from upping the rhetoric.

> The more intransigent they become, the higher they pitch the level of demand, the more it serves to isolate within Pakeha society the liberal-minded group . . . and that I think is a real danger. If that guy [in the Alan Ward lecture] did bring in AK-47s, then that would do two things to Pakeha society. It

would unify it like nothing on earth and it would emasculate what one might call the liberal activists, pro-Treaty, pro-bicultural minority.

And then, Oliver says, you have the very outcome that no one wanted or intended. There's a rhetoric people use, he says, that you see cropping up often in history. They'll say: *If this is not done, then there will be bloodshed*, with no real expectation that things will go that far. 'But the use of that rhetoric tends to be a self-fulfilling prophecy, I think. I think that's where the danger lies.'

Nevertheless, he professes to feel quite hopeful, for the most part. On the one hand he gets the feeling – 'for the time being at least' – that 'Don Brash backed the wrong horse at Orewa.' He also mentions, regarding the Foreshore and Seabed legislation, his respect for Michael Cullen, 'who has the great merit of being once a lecturer in history at the University of Otago. I think he handled this thing with amazing finesse, and I think if the result is a measure which has the National Party saying it surrenders to Maori and has a sizeable number of Maori saying it is confiscation, it can't be too bad'. Dissatisfying the two extremes, he suggests, might indicate that we have a result that New Zealand Pakeha can live with: 'They won't notice it too much.' So long as no one takes some symbolic stand of the kind Margaret Mutu describes?

> Indeed, and that's likely to happen. If that does, that really leads into what I was going to say about the gloomy side of this. That would be one way of polarising and integrating, consolidating [the] Pakeha majority in an anti-Maori way.
>
> The other way, I think is the Maori Party. My guess would be that thanks to the Foreshore and Seabed legislation the Maori Party gains will all be at Labour's expense, so there's at least the possibility that this will throw the government to National and ACT and that would be the worst thing that could happen.

He believes the debate that followed Don Brash's Orewa speech was helpful – and on this, he says, he has differences of opinion with a number of liberal friends. 'I think it was good that things that had been hanging around unrepresented and in a sense disenfranchised were suddenly enfranchised. And to clarify things . . . and I don't think the upshot is at all disastrous.' In that context, he says, notions of AK-47s and blood in the streets and barricades on beaches seem unlikely.

Let's put this in some wider context. Since the end of the Second World War there have been about 122 civil wars. The conventional thinking has been that you have a greater risk of civil war where you have divisions along ethnic or religious lines. But recent research suggests otherwise. According to political scientists David Laitin and James Fearon, in a paper entitled 'Ethnicity, Insurgency and Civil War' in the *American Political Science Review*, it's not ethnic or religious differences that actually tend to be the cause.

There are prosperous, stable countries which have ethnic or religious differences, and yet they hold together. The trouble comes in countries that are impoverished and politically un-stable. Often, the geography will be mountainous – good for guerrilla warfare. And typically, they say, the war won't be over a particular grievance. It's not that grievances are irrelevant, but rather that in the lives of these places, there are nothing *but* grievances.

You'll see fighting break out and the rebels will declare that they've taken action over some particular grievance, but you may well find that if you solve that grievance, you won't bring an end to the fighting. You'll find instead that the 'grievance' was just the most convenient peg to hang their broader objections on.

Now that's not to say that fighting might not break out over specific issues such as economic inequality or the lack of demo-

cracy or civil liberties, or state discrimination against minority
religions or languages, but the data suggests that it's more likely
that the problem will be that you have a large and unstable state
struggling with poverty. There's a checklist they've identified –
if your country fits this profile, you might just be in line for a
civil war:

- extreme poverty – countries with a gross domestic
  product of less than $US6500 per person;
- political instability in new or failing states;
- rough terrain which makes it possible for rebels to hide
  easily;
- large populations;
- external financing.

We have some excellent terrain for guerrilla fighting in this
country, without a doubt, and we are by no means unreliant on
foreign capital. But in any other respect, there's not much there
that strikes a chord.

But just to be safe, what advice can Laitin and Fearon offer a
small stable country in the South Pacific. How might we keep
ourselves out of the way of such a dismal scenario? Would
tolerance for ethnic minorities be recommended? Actually,
although they think it's desirable, they say it's not a magic
bullet for preventing or ending civil war. Establishing ethnic
partitions, though, is a dangerous course, they say, because it
increases the chances of launching an insurgency.

ACT's Stephen Franks sees a few areas where 'you could
cause grave offence' if you set out to implement a *one law for all*
approach. 'But my reading of it is that most Maori have got
much more in common with the rest of us New Zealanders than
they have with some people who've been doing well out of the
grievance industry. We share – we're in sports teams together,

we shop together, we go to church together, we've got a whole lot of interests in common.' If it was handled badly by politicians, though, he can see the possibility of trouble.

Andrew Sharp, professor of Political Studies at the University of Auckland, thinks we're quite capable of avoiding it. What government is for, he says, is peace. 'Peace isn't just lack of war. What it is, is living together in tolerable comfort and being able to sort of confront one another and argue a lot and go away feeling safe. Well, I think we can do that. And that's the way it should be.'

> I think the thing about extremists is their ideas are clearer and if you're a journalist, it's good to write stories about clear ideas. They can articulate what they need. It makes better copy, so naturally journalists do that. Speaking to people in the centre can be very boring because they're too pragmatic, and if you're in government where it really matters, why *would* you trouble yourself with this stuff? Why wouldn't you just set about the normal political job of creating, persuading, and when you can't persuade, legislating your solutions?

The point if you're running things is to take into account the extremes and do what's best for the entire group – be it a council, a business or a nation. You run things from the centre, and you manage the extremists.

We're talking about the notion of a war that no one has said they want. And although Chris Trotter rightly offers that throughout our history the bullets have kept missing, I wonder where the story would have gone if any of them had not. Would a spiral of violence and reprisal have begun, as he suggests, or would we have recoiled in shock?

Perhaps we're not inclined here in New Zealand to that kind of reaction. Perhaps we tend to choose governments that manage to hold the extremes and maintain the peace. And perhaps no one has too little to lose.

Chapter Two

HIGH-WATER MARK

6 February 2035

Wellington

The mood was jubilant today for the first sitting of the Maori Parliament. In contrast to the seventeen days of inauguration ceremonies, today's business was brisk, with only a few formalities preceding the inaugural debate. A bill to ratify the eighth and final Tainui settlement had its first reading, as did one redrawing the jurisdiction boundaries for the Maori District Courts. The self-styled Thorndon Six who have maintained a protest vigil in the trees of Parliament Grounds for sixteen months continued to express their opposition to 'separatist politics'. The six – the last remaining members of the ACT political party which enjoyed a brief flurry of support at the turn of the last century – expressed their determination to remain in the trees until democracy was restored to the voters of New Zealand.

IF YOU'VE ever driven north from Auckland on State Highway One, you'll know that there's no such thing as a building that stretches all the way from Otahuhu to the outskirts of Whangarei. But one afternoon in an Auckland District Court room, in my previous life as a breweries executive, I took the stand to argue just that. I can't remember the finer points of the proposition now but I do know that it was, at first blush, fairly preposterous. Some months earlier I had been chatting with one of our expensive Wellington lawyers about our options for opening a new liquor store in Whangarei. He'd said, Well theoretically, you could do this . . . The more we looked at it, the more confident we got. Under the old liquor laws, it was no easy thing to get a new liquor licence, and it tended to cost you plenty. So instead, taking advantage of some wrinkle in the law, we decided we'd try to redefine the boundaries of a liquor store we had in Otahuhu. We humbly requested the licensing committee, therefore, to declare the boundaries of the store to stretch from Great South Road in Auckland all the way to the site of our Whangarei warehouse. We did our best, and waited a few weeks. Application declined. We shrugged and laughed. Worth a shot, we agreed, and went back to the drawing board.

At law school you learn how to interpret the laws made by judges and the laws made by Parliament, and you learn that it can be a complex and nuanced business. This is an important lesson. You might believe that you have developed a bulletproof interpretation of the law, but if you want to judge its likelihood of success, you'd better ask yourself a question: *Is this interpretation a threat to the established order of things?* If your answer is *Yes*, add several points to the degree of difficulty. Don't imagine, though, that it can't ever happen. There will be times when the court will be quite willing to chip away at the foundations of the status quo.

In 1987, the Court of Appeal was able to do just that. Parliament had included references to the Treaty of Waitangi in its State-Owned Enterprises legislation, and that opened a wide door for the Court. In its judgment, it made observations about the Treaty that would have enormous ramifications. The implements of construction came out and there was an energetic chiselling undertaken upon the status quo. By the time they were done, the Treaty was no longer some historical relic. It had been truly resurrected, and *That Changed*, as the Americans like to say these days, *Everything*.

The Court's judgment raised all kinds of questions for all kinds of people: politicians; public servants; Maori activists and – in principle, if not in practice – all New Zealanders. For some of those parties at least, it launched a new era of debate and interpretation, lobbying and politicking. Not only that, it opened up the possibility that an imaginative thinker might try to interpret the Treaty in new ways. A building might, after all, stretch all the way from South Auckland to Northland.

Theoretically this was a party for everyone, but it would be inaccurate to say that everyone felt like joining in. In truth, the party had already been going quite a while. Since the late sixties when the young Maori activists of Nga Tamatoa had been making their objections known, the media had been reporting the story, but this was not a debate that pleased everyone, if indeed it captured their attention. Whina Cooper had led her Land March, and the country had watched. Historians had published new books asking new questions about the colonisation of New Zealand and some people had read them. The Waitangi Tribunal had been hearing claims and building up a very influential body of findings, which were duly reported but not necessarily widely registered or uniformly welcomed. Radicals like Annette Sykes and Atareta Poananga had been on the TV news uttering inflammatory activist outbursts – and the country had registered those, alright. For the most part, though, this was a debate that only a minority had been actively engaged in.

Margaret Mutu suggests that many Pakeha may not have had much reason to take an interest. They lived comfortably, they had a beautiful country, and by and large they did pretty well. Unlike Maori.

> They watch their Pakeha mates and say: *Well why can't we have what they have?* And so the fact that you are on the back foot in Maoridom forces you to be much more aware of what's going on. And so when the Tribunal does all its work . . . Maoridom takes interest and takes note of what's going on and so we watch and we listen, and when it's in the newspapers we read it and we cut it out because that's really the only way the public gets to know.
>
> Whereas with the Pakeha world I have no doubt they would probably flip across that particular thing, *Oh tribunal something or other*, or *Those Maoris again* and they don't actually read what's there . . . And I think it's not that you haven't been told because the newspapers cover it, the television covers it . . . but it's not going to impinge on you directly because you have faith that even though there were these horrific things that did happen to Maori – and I think by and large . . . your average New Zealander accepts that there were some pretty shoddy things done to Maoridom that were wrong – really nothing's going to happen to you because *We've got a government down there who will make sure that in sorting out this Maori stuff it won't affect any of us.*

It would be inaccurate to say that Pakeha noticed nothing and were not engaged, though. Treaty claims, for example, were huge news in the late '80s and generated any number of vote-winning Winston Peters speeches. But claims were just one facet of the Maori–Pakeha relationship that had to be reconsidered. Other nations with a colonial history were also grappling with broad issues of the rights of indigenous people. Here in New Zealand, uniquely, there was a treaty that seemed, conveniently, to offer a basis for hammering out all the issues that you might need to deal with in this area. The business of recognising the indigenous rights of Maori became the business of interpreting the Treaty. But there were some hooks attached. Some people were interpreting the Treaty to mean that Maori had not ceded sovereignty, which is not a notion that any government is going to be enthusiastic about. It's a rare turkey that will vote for Christmas: *Sorry – our mistake – we'll just withdraw gracefully and let everyone start again.* Little surprise, then, that the Government embraced interpretations of the Treaty that were kinder to the status quo. Maori, they said, signed the Treaty with the undertaking that the Crown would assume sovereignty, and that in return it would guarantee certain rights to Maori, particularly the ones defined in Article Two: tino rangatiratanga.

The whole business of interpreting Article Two is especially interesting. It's not unfeasible to come up with an interpretation in the *warehouse stretching from Auckland to Whangarei* model. Not surprisingly, the government of the time – and each of its successors – plumped for interpretations of a more mild kind. But for all that, one person's mild is another's wild. The Crown tended to go for interpretations of the Treaty which made it clear that it held sovereignty, but in embracing the interpretations it did, it created the conditions for some interesting adventures in policy-making, as Professor Andrew Sharp describes:

> What happened with a lot of the politics of the Maori–Pakeha relationship was that it was, I think, purposefully but not openly left to bureaucratic and legal circles to deal with. And so this meant that points of conflict could be dealt with in the courts, bit by bit, case by case, in a pragmatic way [and by] the bureaucracies and local government in some ways too. So issues of real importance and of fundamental philosophic grounds were left to the courts and bureaucracies and local government to work their way through and didn't get into the public arena.

There was legislation. There were workshops. There were regulations, there were codes of practice. There were new letterheads and logos. There were new programmes, there was new funding. There was plenty going on, and the great preponderance of it was happening in the public sector.

If you happened to be involved, you might be bewildered or bemused by it all, but equally you might be impressed by what you learned about the history of the country you'd grown up in, and a culture you'd known little about. Inevitably there would be mistakes, errors of judgement, waste and rorts. But there would also be change for the better. Treaty claims were settled, new asset bases were established and there were acknowledgements by the Crown that people had been treated wrongly, and had suffered. Programmes and policies were developed that would give many Maori a fresh sense of purpose and pride.

The long and involved process of working out what tino rangatiratanga might mean gave life to a raft of programmes and initiatives, often based in some form or another on ideas of devolution and self-determination. You have a health programme? Let an iwi organise it in their own area. You have an education programme? Perhaps this Maori group will find it works better when they take charge of the programme themselves. *Nothing too sinister, there*, you might think, but of course when you're making taxpayers' money available to people to run programmes of this kind, you're only ever one *Pipi Foundation programme* away from a potential scandal.

Was there a strong clear political strategy to any of this? Not especially. There seemed to be a motivation to *Do The Right Thing*, whatever that might be, in response to the new environment of Treaty thinking, and that took many different forms: accommodating Maori requests for a seat at the table, recognising a right for Maori to be consulted on matters ranging from

Resource Management consents to scientific research, recognition of Treaty principles in legislation and in the practices of public sector organisation, to name just a few.

Whether any of this ever achieved a majority of popular support is debatable, and given that it was left to the courts and the public sector to implement, the opportunity to test it in the electoral process was limited. Chris Trotter maintains the issue was captured by an elite of politicians, public servants, academics, commentators and vested interests, and that for as long as there was a consensus across the political parties to stick to the mission, the voter had little say in the matter. But that came to an abrupt halt when Don Brash gave his speech at Orewa and the subsequent polls told the story of a disaffected public.

> What we saw in reaction to Brash's speech was a very powerful warning, I think, to the elites, to the Wellington elites, which was: *Pull back*. And Clark heard them. She did this amazing handbrake turn: 180 degrees, and smoking tyres in the other direction. She understands our constitution quite well and is very respectful of majorities.

But was the Government also a little relieved to be making the U-turn? If you consider the way in which it had rejected recent Waitangi Tribunal findings on minerals, airwaves and the foreshore, it was clearly feeling uncomfortable with the direction in which some Treaty interpretations were heading.

The question we're left with is: Has the high tide come in for this era of policy-making? Is that as far as you can expect policy to go in interpreting the Treaty in favour of Maori rights? And if it is, how might you expect Maori to respond to that? Does a so-called Treaty Industry wither away if the Government does a U-turn? (Of course, that assumes a U-turn took place. The Government is more likely to argue that they're simply holding firm where they are.) In this chapter and the next, we'll consider the two directions the tide can move from here. Let's begin by asking what you might see if the tide were to come in further.

Consider what Ani Mikaere had to say in the 2004 Bruce Jesson Memorial Lecture: for Pakeha to gain legitimacy here, she said, it is they who must place their trust in Maori, not the other way around. 'It is the wronged party who is being expected to submit to terms imposed by the wrongdoer.'

> I regard tikanga as the first law of Aotearoa. It arrived here with our ancestors and it operated effectively to serve their needs for a thousand years before Pakeha came. It was the only system of law in operation when the first Pakeha began living here amongst us. Had the reaffirmation of Maori authority in the second article of Te Tiriti o Waitangi been adhered to, the relationship between Pakeha and Maori would have been regulated by tikanga Maori throughout our shared history. I believe it would have resulted in a far healthier relationship than the one we currently have.

She frankly acknowledged to questioners afterwards that what she aspired to was perhaps a faint hope. Still, she maintained that if Pakeha really want to feel they belong they need to take a leap of faith, and submit to the first law of the land.

Assuming for a moment (one giant leap in itself) that the nation might be willing to take the leap, what implications might that have? If we let tikanga Maori regulate our lives what will happen? What, for starters, does tikanga Maori mean, exactly? Margaret Mutu points out that it reflects the accumulated wisdom of people who have been living here the longest:

> Tikanga is very much something which is built up on what we consider anyway to be just centuries and centuries of common sense, of learning what works in certain circumstances. That's why tikanga is specific to particular areas because what works in one area won't work in another area. Because of the

geographic locale, the people who are there, the history of the place, all sorts of factors.

So tikanga's very much like that, and tikanga will allow that if you get another community coming in that has found it can live by a different set of tikanga that is not a problem, provided when they are in my locale they adhere to my tikanga so that they don't upset the balance while they're in my area.

If Pakeha wish to come in, and they have their own ways of doing things, that's fine and that's the big difference I think there is between the English culture as such and the Maori culture, and the Polynesian cultures as well. We're very happy to accommodate, whereas the English culture is . . . very monocultural, and as far as they're concerned the only right way is their way . . . and it's not helpful. It doesn't allow people to be who they are, basically, which to us means it lacks a lot of common sense.

When Maori use this kind of talk, though, about Maori law taking precedence, people get uneasy. *Where will it end*, people fret: *they'll want to kick us out.* Margaret Mutu says they should stop worrying.

We can't, we invited them in here. And we married into them ... when you've got a guest who misbehaves as badly as these people misbehave, but they're still there, I mean sure you could kick them out but you can't in practice, you can't kick them out. So you've got to try and find a way of working around it. All you can do is call on their laws, and that's what we've always done. We've said: *Well now, come on, you know this was ours and you took it against your own laws, so you're going to have to fix that up.*

In theory, the notion of two laws contending for priority looks problematic. In practice, we've actually managed to incorporate the one into the other, on occasion. Aspects of the Resource Management Act, for example, incorporate tikanga Maori.

So what are the odds of the leap of faith taking place? Slim, one would think. It's not hard to see the current backlash making things tougher. It's not hard to see the courts and the public service losing some of their capacity to develop policies on the Maori–Pakeha relationship. But that wouldn't be the end of the line for anyone who wanted to argue for these policies. Even with those other avenues closed there's still another very good one: Parliament.

Which brings us nicely to the Maori Party. What do they want, and when do they want it? If you want to get a handle on where the tide might reach if it were to wash higher, you'll get a useful idea from looking at the policies of this party.

Tariana Turia, in her first speech in Parliament as co-leader of the Maori Party said: 'the best form of leadership for Maori-dom is Maoridom. We need to seek leadership from within, find the inspiration that exists in our people'. And she amplified that in a column in early 2005, pointing out that: 'Self-determination is not a dirty word.'

> In some stages of self-determination, separation may indeed be a vital part of the process. Just as the All Blacks head off to a training camp, or religious leaders take themselves off on a retreat, so too indigenous initiatives may also require a sustained period of focus and self-concentration in order to assert and confirm our roles as tangata whenua.
>
> We should not be afraid of different paths of development. In personal relationships, occasional separation from each other can be mutually beneficial for both partners. It provides a vital opportunity to build one's strength, to focus on our assets, and to be recharged, and re-energised. It also enables both partners to gain some perspective on the relationship – to respect the different needs of each partner instead of losing sight of our uniqueness.
>
> I am intolerant of the knocker mentality, of those who want to criticise or denigrate progress because it is different than the expectations they have. Just because one is FOR something, doesn't have to mean we are AGAINST everything else.

It intrigues me that whenever I have stood up loud and proud for Maori, that opponents will think what I'm really saying is to put down others. We can love apples and pears, we can flourish in our own separate authority, and still appreciate the diversity of the mix; tangata whenua can be self-determining as well as any other New Zealander, and we should commend that initiative rather than knocking it.

What that means in policy terms is not necessarily reservations and separate courts and parliaments. It could – theoretically – but in practice it seems much more likely that the party will argue for more of what's been working (mostly) successfully already: devolution. What seems most likely is that you'll see the party arguing for more funding of entities run *by* Maori *for* Maori. A huge amount – the party President, Professor Whatarangi Winiata has argued – is spent on Maori every year:

> The Maori partner has little to say about how much the appro-priations should be, what the policies should be, how policies are to be implemented and how policies and their managers are to be evaluated. But this partner gets the blame for poor performance.

You can probably also expect to hear more of the concept developed by Professor Winiata of a three-house parliament: one Maori house, one Pakeha house, and an upper house. But interestingly, his view on that has lately evolved. He said at the end of a lecture in early 2005 that he would put the two 'lower' houses of the three-house model 'into the one house that we know as Parliament'.

> This prescription is being opportunistic in light of the new phenomenon on the political scene – a distinctly Maori politi-cal party with a constitution, policies and practices that are kaupapa driven with the real possibility of having sufficient representation in Parliament to be influential in that context.

The Maori Party, jointly with all other parties, would be respon-
sible for kawanatanga *and* rangatiratanga, with the latter having
a greater presence than it has had for nearly two centuries.

None of this should be terribly unnerving to anyone willing to
listen to an alternative point of view, surely. Chris Trotter
welcomes the notion of these issues being put before the
country. Societies, he says, are at their healthiest when they are
debating these issues and putting them before legislatures and
risking loss:

> I remember a long streak of a guy with a great shock of woolly
> hair down in Dunedin who wanted the marijuana laws
> reformed. He wanted decriminalisation of marijuana as a
> controlled drug. I remember him going to his first regional
> conference and the people looking at him askance. He stood up
> there and he made his argument and a couple of us backed him
> up and it went down in a screaming heap as you'd expect; but
> he came back the next year and it went down in a screaming
> heap, but not quite such a screaming heap and this time there
> were two or three more people who came up to back him at the
> microphone; the third year lots of people came up to back him
> at the microphone, he had been indefatigable. He had sent
> around his pamphlets and his papers and he'd sent round
> references to journals, and by the fourth year, only at regional
> council level certainly, it passed.
>
> And I have never forgotten that. That is democracy. That is
> how you do it. You win them over a year at a time. And I have
> never forgotten that example, when you are wanting something
> radical to happen, you mustn't ever just use institutional power
> to assert your will because you ain't gonna be in control of those
> institutions forever. And someone can do the opposite as soon
> as they get their hands on that power. Whereas if you persuade
> a majority, then it's a lot harder to turn back.

If the notion of the tide of Treatyism washing higher seems
unsettling, consider this thought: these people are going about

things in a remarkably conventional way for scary radicals. They want power *sharing*. They want to debate this in Parliament. They had a hikoi of 20,000 that marched peaceably down Lambton Quay, stood at the doors of Parliament, made their point and went home. No violence, no disorder. And this despite the fact that according to many who were interviewed, they were marching because they were – justifiably or not – feeling disrespected and disregarded.

We don't know yet what the Maori Party's chances will be of winning popular support for any of these policies. In the first-past-the-post electoral system, the tyranny of the majority worked against you. The aspirations of – say – 15 per cent of the electorate risked being voted down by 85 per cent. That in part explains the policy-making of the last two decades that went on outside the scrutiny of Parliament. In an MMP system, though, your few votes can carry amply more heft – with the important qualification that you can get punished for over-playing that hand. The potential is there, then, for the Maori Party to keep up the momentum on Treaty policy, notwith-standing handbrakes or U-turns by the present government.

What may also help the party is the developing trend in Parliament to legislate more specifically on this issue. 'Treaty Principles' which have enjoyed so much enthusiastic press lately tended to be very broad and abstract. The great advantage to doing things that way was that Parliament could pass legislation that used a vague phrase: *shall have regard to the principles of the Treaty of Waitangi* without having to reach any sort of agreement on what it meant – *We'll just leave it to the courts*. More recently, a different approach has emerged. The idea is that you draft very specifically to the extent that – if you're talking about health funding, for example, you might draft something along the lines of: *this kind of provider will be entitled to this kind of support if they are working in this particular field of care to provide such and such a service.*

If you can reach agreement on things at that level of specificity it becomes possible for Tariana Turia, for example, to talk about the particular examples she's seen of provider funding working with a given group of patients in a given area with a given outcome. If she can argue it that way, the objections in principle to the idea of 'separatist' policies tend to be blunted in the face of the good it constitutes in practice. Very pragmatic, very much more persuasive. She gets to argue for a form of self-determination as you might expect according to tino rangatiratanga, but if she does so at a pragmatic level, the chances of getting support for the strategy are much better.

It bears thinking a little about the reason people advocate these Treaty Industry policies. Cynics maintain it's a self-serving gravy train. They're bound to be right to some extent. Every worthy cause attracts its freeloaders and its parasites. But if you disqualified any government practice on that basis, you'd have no ACC, no immigration, no education, and in fact hardly a government activity left standing. The more important question to ask is: How much benefit does the policy bring about? Anyone who frets that the whole business is too unaccountable should be pleased at the prospect of a Maori Party in Parliament. They will inevitably be promoting legislation on the subject, and it should be possible to hold the policies and their consequent activities to no end of scrutiny. If there's a rort in there, any half-dozen MPs should be ready to spot it.

It would be nice to think that when that happens, the context for the debate will not be one that sees Maori simply as some kind of liability. Hekia Parata bemoans the tendency for the tail to wag the dog:

New Zealand has one of the highest imprisonment rates in the world and that totals about 6000 people, of whom 2900 are Maori. If you think about it, there's 500- or 600,000 Maori, total, so we've got 2900 Maori prisoners and 497,100 or 597,100 who aren't.

It's all one-dimensional, so you could forgive all New Zealanders, Maori and non-Maori alike, sighing every time they hear there's another Maori story because that's what they get dished up. We don't get dished up the bountiful stories of productive families who are working really hard and doing their best to educate their kids and then being successful. That is something that Te Puni Kokiri is on this pathway now of talking about: Maori succeeding as Maori; exploring Maori potential rather than Maori disparity; giving energy to all the positive constructive stories about Maori and the areas for opportunity.

She recalls her first awareness that being Maori wasn't necessarily an attractive option. 'I grew up in a community and in a family where I had explicitly been told how fortunate I was to be Ngati Porou and Ngai Tahu and to be bilingual and bicultural and so forth – and it wasn't until I think I went away to senior high school that I discovered that not everybody thought that.'

That was amazing to me at sixteen to discover that people had a different view of it and that it was a more derogatory view. I took quite a while to come to terms with that . . . people decide that you look Maori, therefore you are Maori, therefore you must be in support of the Treaty settlements process and therefore you're getting a handout.

Within Maori of course, we tend to start categorising by tribes. Traditionally we have been at loggerheads about this or we've been in sympathy with each other and therefore we are gonna react to each other in this particular way. I think in New Zealand, for some reason, we've got such a commitment to conformity that where anyone is different it challenges the sense of balance or assurance that other people have. It is just an implicit challenge. So . . . when we say we're all New Zealanders, which of course we are, I've always said: *Yes we are, but we are just not all the same New Zealanders and nor should we be. We've got such a rich set of his and her stories to draw on.*

Whatever you think of the quality or worthiness or appropriateness of the policies that have emerged over the past thirty years, you would have hard work demonstrating that many Maori are not in a better position today than they were a generation ago. The diversity amongst Maori that Hekia Parata describes is clear enough amongst the accomplished young Maori who are emerging more qualified and more ready than their parents' generation to tackle new ventures and take their people in new directions.

When people like development-oriented Maori leader Shane Jones argue that Maori need to move on from grievance mode and grasp the opportunities open to them, they find a positive response among young Maori. You sometimes get the sense, though, that some Pakeha interpret that as an argument for assimilation. It's hard to imagine that's what Shane Jones contemplates, and it's not how Hekia Parata sees it either:

> There are lots of Maori people involved in being Maori and also making choices about their children going to kohanga reo or going to kura kaupapa and what not, while running their small businesses and being part of their whanau, and we need those stories to be more obviously available – because otherwise we just get presented negatively on the news.

As we'll see in the next chapter, there seems to be an assimilationist urge behind this *one law for all* point of view. If people imagine that there are only a few Maori who will mind if the tide goes out on a culture that is more vibrant today than it has been in decades, they are probably in for a disappointment.

Margaret Mutu looks out fifty years and hopes for more understanding 'that every New Zealander will be equally as comfortable in the Maori world as Maori are in the Pakeha world. And half of the horribleness that you have seen in the last two years in particular I am sure would just melt. That's what I'd love to see'.

Chapter Three

25 April 2015

Tauranga

The Treaty of Waitangi was formally incinerated today outside the National Archives in Tauranga. It was the concluding event in a week of remembrance for the Wellington Earthquake of 2011. President Winston Peters noted that even the darkest of clouds could have a silver lining. 'That earthquake, dreadful though it was, emptied out the so-called academic and policy-making elite and cleared the way for some much-needed plain thinking in this country.' He said it was a day of profound significance for the Republic, and he congratulated Prime Minister Rich for achieving the parliamentary support necessary to consign a divisive document to the shadows of history.

DON BRASH'S speech to the Orewa Rotary Club was a clever piece of writing. It contained enough substance to justify the argument that he was expressing his considered and passionately held beliefs. But it also gave him the lines he needed to strike a chord with the voter who might not feel burdened by the need to give those arguments much thought. *I know what's wrong with this bloody country, alright. Don't need to hear all the details. Just a few of the right statements will do nicely, thanks. Right behind you on this one, Don.*

The formula is effective, but that doesn't make it admirable. It polarises, and it leaves scarcely anyone better informed. It validates people's intolerance, it gives them permission to cling to prejudices, and it gives succour to closed minds.

In the Orewa speech Brash fretted about a 'dangerous drift towards racial separatism in New Zealand'. There could be 'no basis for special privileges for any race, no basis for government funding based on race, no basis for introducing Maori wards in local authority elections, and no obligation for local govern-ments to consult Maori in preference to other New Zealanders'.

Alarming indeed. The problem was, the diagnosis bore only the barest resemblance to the patient's actual symptoms. This was misrepresentation and overstatement of a most cynical kind. The 'privileges' and funding, I argued in *Bullshit, Backlash & Bleeding Hearts*, were slight in monetary terms, were founded on constructive principles, and were yielding results that stood to benefit everyone. The obligation to consult – and the creation of Maori wards – had a sound pragmatic basis and simply ensured that Maori had a voice amongst many others. You could only interpret this to mean that Maori were being given the 'whip hand' if you made some effort to ignore the facts of the matter.

But a winning formula has its seductive appeal, and clearly this one still holds its lustre for the man who would like to be Prime Minister. So at the beginning of election year, he found another outrage to share with the nation. He told a business lunch in Auckland that knowledge of the Treaty and its 'supposed' principles would not be a condition of employment under a National-led government. 'We know that almost every advertisement for a job in a government department still includes words noting that the department has a *commitment to the principles of the Treaty of Waitangi*, though without the slightest explanation of what that might mean,' he said. His government would adopt a 'less exotic' approach to recruiting public servants – it would seek auditors who could audit, managers who could manage and accountants who could count. Nothing like a dose of no-nonsense common-sense talk to get the business audience on side.

But let's not forget that these auditors and managers and accountants will be working in government. Would it not be a good idea to make sure they're familiar with the way our system of government works? And how far would you say you would get in a description of the way our system of government works before you got into a discussion about the Treaty?

This kind of consideration gets lost when you're going for the cheap shot. No doubt some of the people writing these job advertisements are slotting in a ritual Treaty acknowledgement without much thought, but sloppy copywriting is hardly enough reason to discredit a valid employment issue.

And so it continues to go. There are robust objections you can mount to aspects of the 'Treaty Industry' – and we'll consider some of those shortly – but these are not, for the most part, the ones Dr Brash has been offering. People have an absolute democratic right to choose not to be bothered by any alternative point of view. Politicians have an absolute democratic right to massage those people with the reassurance that they needn't bother looking for one. But how much good will it do anybody?

Dr Brash can assert that our preoccupation with the Treaty is taking us down a dangerous road, but the specific examples he's offered don't do very much to prove it. Some people take a more optimistic view, Hekia Parata for one, who was herself a candidate in Wellington Central for the party Dr Brash now leads. She thinks the Treaty held, and still holds, the potential for us to make a better place.

> I know this sounds extremely Pollyanna-ish but I am a child of a bicultural setting, of families and so forth. And it's all been opportunity for me. I've been given the opportunity of a dual perspective, a dual set of values and beliefs; the opportunity to create a third set of values and beliefs out of that, as have my children in turn. I've been brought up with the expectation that this is a country of wealth and of opportunity that I can contribute to and gain from.

There seems to be an assumption propping up the *one law for all New Zealanders* argument that we all peer out at the world through the same pair of spectacles: that we all have the same expectations, and we all live our lives in the same way. Only a little reflection should tell us that our contemporary society doesn't look anything like that. Take this example from Linda Papuni that *Reality* magazine offered in a discussion of the Seabed and Foreshore debate:

> My story is of hot bright summer days on the white sandy beaches around Gisborne, where we played, swam and picnicked; days filled with fun and laughter. Then my Pakeha mother died and my world changed.
>
> My Maori father introduced another way of being on the beach. The beaches we now visited were rocky and we gathered seafood to supplement the family's meagre income. Gone were the sun umbrellas and balls. Sacks and kits for gathering seafood were the norm.
>
> We were taught to observe the proper ways of doing things in the sea. Our behaviour was considered – there was no yelling or laughter. We went about the collecting of seafood in an orderly and quiet manner. I was always embarrassed to think that Pakeha might be watching me, that people who knew me might see me having to collect food from the beach.

While for Pakeha 'beach' is lifestyle, for Maori 'beach' in many cases is subsistence living and this is especially so in rural, coast-bound communities where our people's survival depends on gathering food from the beach as we have always done.

Maori and Pakeha live in different worlds. Maori collecting seafood should not have to contend with SUVs and boat-trailers driving up and down beaches contributing to the destruction of our pipi beds and the habitats of other sea creatures.

Today's level of mobility has enabled Pakeha to go to places they would never have considered going prior to the late-1960s. Maori have had to share their beaches without complaint. The putting up of signs and gates should not come as a surprise to people, especially if we consider the erosion of our beaches.

Conscious that my Pakeha relations and friends have an interest in the preservation of our sea and landscapes, my hope is that by telling our stories we can find a workable future alongside one another.

If 'one law for all' represents some kind of urge to assimilate people with a different perspective into just one standard white-bread view of the world, it's hard to see the effort yielding anything but resentment and objections. The most sensitive question that raises, as we saw in preceding chapters, is: Could that drive people to violence? That seems only a remote prospect. But it's hard to see how it could not have a demoralising effect and be counter-productive at a time when a Maori renaissance is yielding more graduates, more new business, and an exciting time of cultural growth.

It's hard too, to avoid the feeling that there's some contradictory thinking involved here, as Ani Mikaere pointed out in her Jesson lecture:

> When travelling overseas, Pakeha leap forward to perform bastardised versions of the haka and 'Pokarekare Ana', and adorn themselves with Maori pendants in an attempt to identify

themselves as New Zealanders: when in Aotearoa it is often those same people who decry any assertion of Maori language and culture as a threat to their identity.

Looking forward, then, how much room will there be for diversity if Dr Brash has his way? Interesting question; because for all the grand talk about *putting an end to all this nonsense*, there was quite a lot of equivocating going on in 2004 as interviewers asked him to nominate any particular aspects of 'privilege' or 'preferential treatment' for Maori he would shut down. The tide might not necessarily go out as far as the bold words imply. It's possible, of course, that he's already had something of the result he was looking for. His poll surge, as Chris Trotter argues, had a chilling effect on the present administration's policies, and the consequence could be that whichever administration holds office in the next term, the tide might not move very far in either direction.

But that's not to say that other politicians, given some future opportunity, might not have more of an appetite for the truly bold measure. That might carry the tide back out quite some way. Let's consider some of the arguments they've been making. ACT MP Stephen Franks thinks we're on the wrong track in a variety of ways. He cites the debate over genetic engineering as an example, where he was on a committee with Nanaia Mahuta:

> The Royal Commission said it was going to go around the country to ascertain the Maori view on genetic engineering. And I said to Nanaia, *Why? My grandparents would never have pretended they had any cultural views on GE because no one knew about it. Why would Maori have a view on GE? This is all novel – it has to be thought through.* And Nanaia laughed and said: *No, it's what you do today, isn't it?* And I said: *Well is there a Maori religious view on these things, on genetic engineering?*

No, he recalls her saying, *She really didn't know*. When she came back and reported, he asked her about it.

> I said: *You said there's no Maori opinion on these things*. She said: *Well what do you think would happen if someone comes around and solemnly asks what your religious view is of these matters, of course you are going to feel you ought to have one*. And so we watched the development of a creed in the space of a few months. It suddenly became an article of faith that Maori have a view about these matters.

Who wouldn't do that, he asks. 'This isn't saying Maori are children, but – it's just like anything, if you want to taint evidence, you go along as if you expect the people to know, kids or any group . . . you go along as if you expect there's something they know and look as if you'll be disappointed if they don't.'

> I think that a lot of Maori spirituality, when we were growing up, was bloody obvious. It was a very pious form of High Catholicism and there's relics of that still, but there's a whole overlay of reconstructing. Then again, I go back to Scotland, in the same way that the Scots reconstructed the whole of Scottish custom because upper-class poms were fascinated by the tartan and Queen Victoria thought it was very romantic to know about Scottish history. You have the creation of ersatz Scottishness. That's been well documented. The heraldic tartans are a modern creation and I think we're busy doing that.

There's a related aspect to this, and that's been apparent in some of the debate over, for example, taniwha holding up roading projects. Our courts try to take a rationalist, secular approach. They try to leave spirituality out of the equation. If a court is forced to confront an issue like a taniwha, it will tend to say something like: Look, we respect any person's right to pursue their faith, but we can't explore that faith and try and prove it in any rationalist way because it cannot be done, and it simply can't be accommodated in this court.

Chris Trotter says you can turn the line of an old Joni Mitchell song back on itself. Rather than *You don't know what you've got till it's gone*, he says, it sometimes pays to consider that you forget *How much you didn't like the way things used to be*.

> It was a long hard struggle to get religion out of the law. And to put it back, I think, is just insane. But people forget. If you haven't had it for a generation you don't know what it's like to grow up in a society where individual liberty is constrained by religious bigotry, then perhaps it's easy to think it would be a good idea to have religious views given the force of law. But I think a New Zealand court would be very loath to put a motorway through a Maori burial ground, just as in the end it was very difficult to put a motorway through the Bolton Street cemetery in Wellington, for exactly the same reason: that the idea of disturbing the dead in any culture is taboo. And so it should be. That weight to one's ancestors has got to be recognised even in the most secular, scientific of societies because those links are impossible to underestimate.
>
> But if someone was to say *You can't put a road through there because there's a dragon that lives in that cave*, people would go: *A dragon? Really? And where did you buy that LSD, and how can I get some?* The taniwha is a Maori dragon and I don't really see the need in a utilitarian sense to recognise dragons.

Trotter sees in people like Tariana Turia, an attempt to recapture the whole religious/Maori scientific world-view:

> To me, it sits strangely in the twenty-first century and I don't think it's viable. In a world of computers and satellites, talking about *Papatuanuku* seems as quaint as talking about *Zeus* does to me. You couldn't rebuild the religion of ancient Greece or the religion of the Anglo-Saxons now without looking as silly as Himmler did when he tried to do the thing in Germany in the thirties. It just looks bizarre.

If you're not careful, good intentions can carry you well into the realm of foolishness, to be sure. But there's a tendency in debates over issues such as this to hold up an absurdity and use it to justify scrapping an entire policy. Do we contemplate scrapping the system of tax deductions on the basis that some people make outrageous claims for deductions they're not entitled to?

Maori may not have an opinion on a particular issue, but it would be quite wrong to say that they hold no opinion on any matter. The thinking behind the Resource Management Act recognised that. Tribunal decisions such as Motunui had shown quite clearly that there were aspects of the environment that were very important to Maori. You don't run a sewerage outfall onto traditional fishing grounds. You don't go developing on top of sacred burial grounds. You should make due allowance for cultural values. You should talk to people of the area and establish that whatever you're doing does no harm of that kind.

Tikanga, Margaret Mutu pointed out, is built up on accumulated common sense – a knowledge as to what works in certain circumstances. It's specific to particular areas. It can help.

You inevitably strike anomalies and errors as you settle in with a new system. We've already had to contend with issues of apparent 'greenmail', and claims that have seemed at first blush to be preposterous, and yes, taniwha holding up roading projects. But it's hardly unknown for a system to be adjusted and calibrated as it goes along. It seems to make far more sense to go on tuning the system of consultation than to throw it out altogether.

It's certainly possible that if you were to give the system free rein and make no changes as you went along, you might see some kind of newly constructed creed accumulating influence over time. But why would we break with the habit of a lifetime?

We constantly tinker with policy and adjust it. It's hard to see this one being left to run itself.

Consultation is just one of a number of issues that attract criticism. Consider the 'moral mortgage'. This is an argument that we will never be allowed to stop being guilty and saying sorry for what happened to Maori. This, we're told, divides us. How much merit is there in the argument?

Bill Oliver points out that if you consider the greater sweep of New Zealand history since colonisation, the Treaty has meant nothing to the dominant group and there is at least the possibility that historians in 100 years time will think: Why did that curious blip occur in the 1980s that died out in 2010? 'We have to remember in our short history as a mixed society, the prominent element has not ignored but has paid inadequate, or belittling or minimising attention to Maori, the minority element.'

Given that the weight of history tends to be on the side of the dominant group, it's hard to see why people in that group get quite so exercised about this. It hasn't been going on that long. We have been going through a process of claims, but if you think the focus is going to remain on claims and griev-ances, consider the Hui Taumata – the Maori Development Summit – in Wellington in March 2005, where talk was all about enterprise and not about honouring the Treaty and claims; and consider how people like Business Roundtable Chairman Rob McLeod have been talking. He said that if the unemployment and income gaps between Maori and Pakeha were closed, an extra $41 billion would be pumped into the Maori economy – far more than Treaty settlements would ever deliver.

The emphasis has been placed, instead, on education and skills. There was a strong theme coming out of the hui that the primary goal for Maori needs to shift from gaining access and participation, to pursuing quality and achievement.

Now you could say that this new focus has come about because a much-needed backlash jolted people out of their old attitudes. Don't be so sure. Respect, resources and renaissance helped bring this about. And don't be too quick to assume that this might diminish the significance of the Treaty. Talk at the hui suggests that it still matters a good deal.

We'll see in the next chapter that there's an argument that many of the issues that have been dealt with through the Treaty might have been more easily dealt with in a different way. Before we consider that, though, we also need to consider the objections many people – politicians in particular – raise about the way the Treaty has been interpreted, in particular the question of its 'so-called' principles.

A fundamental issue is sovereignty: how much did Maori sign away, and how much did they believe they were signing away? Chris Trotter disagrees with the proposition that the Maori would never have granted 2000 people the right to rule over 60- or 80,000:

> If a nation has suffered as Maori suffered in the 1810s, '20s and '30s, they may very well surrender their sovereignty to a super-power that is perceived as having the weaponry, the organisation, the wisdom and the spiritual guidance . . .

He sees the Treaty as being a way of 'bringing an end to the slaughter and of bringing in the hope of a better way of organising life, and of the protection of this extraordinary state, with its laws and its ships and cannons and men in strange attire'.

> You are talking about people coming together at Waitangi for the last twenty to thirty years who have been involved in terrible

wars. It was like Europe at the end of World War Two. There were just people going backwards, forwards, moving – no one had any sense of security at all.

Stephen Franks suggests that Maori understanding of ranga-tiratanga has been misinterpreted. He thinks it was expressing the English concept of *your home is your castle*, which was revolutionary, because in Maori society 'your home wasn't a sanctuary at all'. Here was a promise that 'even the King cannot come onto your land without a search warrant'.

> That's a *revolutionary* thing, a way of trying to describe what property meant, and it was quite recently evolved to that state in 1840. I think when you look at the text there you can see a large reflection of the missionaries' fear that property rights would turn into [what happened in Scotland] where they were conferred on the chiefs and the chiefs then sold their people out and the clearances took place.

Look at the language, Franks points out, it's quite peculiar because it said that rangatiratanga was extended to all the ordinary people.

> Now what could that mean in Maori terms? I think the words were doing something odd. If rangatiratanga was defining chieftainship and the rights of self-government within your land, rangatiratanga would have been the powers of the chiefs, but what they said was, rangatiratanga . . . accrues to ordinary people.

It's really interesting, he says, that you would be telling the ordinary people that they get rangatiratanga. The term 'exclusive possession' he points out, is just a classical statement of property law as the British knew it – your right to use it, enjoy it and dispose of it.

> So I have never found Article Two very complex, but this is a non-historian looking at it, really a lawyer, thinking *These guys*

*were writing a legal document. What did they think they were
doing?* And that's another reason why I find the more elaborate
versions of taonga a little bit fanciful, because no lawyer of that
period would have ever dreamed of trying to give exclusive
possession to something like language. I mean a language for a
start: if it's exclusive it's not usable.

Those early property lawyers, he says, were very conscious of
how hard it is to create genuine property interests in things that
aren't readily capable of identification. He thinks it's 'highly
unlikely' that they thought of taonga as more than the guns, the
valuables, the trade goods and so on.

> I don't have a problem with Article Two. I think Article Two is
> a very sound basis for saying: *You'll own your property and
> within it we can't come in there and interfere with the way you are
> living.*

If you take a narrower interpretation of Article One and Article
Two, you get a significantly different result. If you conclude that
Maori yielded sovereignty without reservation and were guar-
anteed a narrower parcel of rights, it becomes much harder to
argue for a number of things. For example, it becomes harder to
argue that Maori are entitled to rights of self-determination
under Article Two. It becomes harder to make the case – as the
Waitangi Tribunal has done – that the expression 'taonga'
embraces language, for example, or airwaves, or intellectual
property.

If the 'tide' goes out, this may be where politicians begin
looking to make some changes. Of course, some politicians are
ready to make some changes right now. Consider the Hon.
Winston Peters, and his private member's bill to remove Treaty
references from all legislation. A rival MP said the man had the
'luck of the devil' to get his bill drawn from the ballot in an
election year.

Lucky or not, the bill will make things interesting. It's the bluntest of instruments: it simply removes from all of the Acts of Parliament of New Zealand those sections or subsections which contain the expressions 'the principles of the Treaty'; 'the principles of the Treaty of Waitangi'; and 'Treaty of Waitangi and its principles.' To do that it removes no less than a whole (and not the least bit unimportant) section from the Resource Management Act, and clauses and sections from statutes as varied as the Education Act, the Royal New Zealand Foundation for the Blind Act and the Historic Places Act.

What does Peters have against these words? According to the explanatory note, quite a few objections, actually. They include the following:

- Parliament never actually defined them. Instead they left the job to judges who – and you may find the logic a little tricky to follow here – have been increasingly activist and liberal in defining them but have also left them after two decades 'largely undefined and ambiguous'.

- They're legal catnip. (And here we can see that this particular lawyer is not compromised by any feelings of professional solidarity.) The principles 'have become a source of ongoing litigation regarding their relevance and meaning', benefiting the lawyers, but not Maori. Nevertheless, even though Maori have seen no money, it seems this activity has 'surreptitiously created unrealistic expectations among Maori in relation to their entitlements from society'.

- They have created a diversion. The pathway to success for both Maori and non-Maori lies elsewhere. We should have ignored their siren song.

- They have warped the thinking of some Maori. Treaty principles can encourage you to portray yourself as a victim, constantly in grievance mode.

- And finally, they are divisive, and not in any lightweight way. He frets that we might, if we're not careful, go down the same destructive path of separate development that South Africa chose last century.

Well, checkmate and all that. There are two excellent words you can deploy in a debate if you want to close it down: cry 'Nazi' or 'Apartheid' and you have a good chance of clearing the field.

What's most exasperating about this is that it takes a valid criticism and amplifies it into something vastly broader, deeper and ostensibly more sinister or dangerous than it ever was. Say this kind of thing in the abstract, and people, wanting to believe the worst, will swallow it. But start talking about the particular reasons people take particular cases to court, and you find that there's actually a perfectly sound reason for doing what they're doing. In the famous *Lands* case, for example, the NZ Maori Council were worried that land that was subject to Treaty claims would be sold off by the Government before claims could be heard. So they went to court, relying on the notoriously broad section 9 of the State-Owned Enterprises Act – the defining example, possibly, of an undefined Treaty principles clause. Yes, its ambiguity opened up a challenging new legal chapter, and yes, the fact that the courts were left to work things out created a degree of uncertainty. But the notion that the whole field is some kind of expanding black hole is just plain wrong.

In particular, the panic-mongering overlooks the fact that Parliament, in recent instances, has been remedying the deficiency by legislating much more specifically. The option is open to Parliament at any time to amend any of the offending legislation to be more specific. Any statute that presently refers to Treaty principles can be amended to state more specifically what should be done in that particular legislation to ensure you're not breaching your Treaty obligations. You can have the debate right there and then about what those obligations might be in the particular circumstances, and worry no more about what the courts might try – years later – to deduce you had in mind. More importantly, you'll have that debate with MPs who take the point of view that it's not a bad thing to frame your legislation in a way that satisfies whatever principles you consider the Treaty of Waitangi to contain.

That's important, because while Peters and a number of his parliamentary colleagues might have no truck with the 'Treaty Industry' there is a significant number of MPs who beg to differ. There's little doubt that this is a debate that needs to be had, but Peter's strategy here is pure politics. This kind of legislation is little more than a wild theatrical flailing with a machete, bringing down whatever should happen to lie in the path of the MP's mighty swing. It has the political advantage of appearing to bring down the wrath of the righteous on the Treaty gravy train, while being inevitably doomed to failure for lack of numbers in the House. The government, to Peter's satisfaction, then wears the opprobrium from his righteous supporters for thwarting his noble cause.

Chris Trotter points out another risk to the strategy of inserting broad principles in the law and leaving it to the courts to sort out – you might win the battle but lose the war if you rely on the courts to do what Parliament will not. If you do that, he says, 'all you are saying to your opponents is: *get control of the judiciary*'.

And that is what the Republicans in the United States have done. They have got control. They are about to completely transform the Supreme Court and that will, for a whole generation, mean that extreme right-wing viewpoints are at the summit of the American judiciary and that's . . . the consequence of using judicial methods in preference to legislative methods. I think probably the greatest moment for American democracy in the last fifty years was when Lyndon Johnson went to the Congress and said *We shall overcome* and passed the Civil Rights Act.

That's the way you do it. You convince the majority. You shame them into doing the right thing. And, you know, you don't rely on judges, you argue it out. And I just think, the principles of the Treaty and the way they have been inserted in legislation is just a basic plea to the judiciary to do what they dare not do themselves. And if you haven't carried the majority with you, the majority will react with great vehemence against that; they will say you've got unelected people to do what you elected people wouldn't do, that's not on. So they'll find a way to get around that.

Peters has a point, it must be said, about the way in which these shadowy and unknowable Treaty principles have diverted some Maori. The fact is, over the past two decades the Treaty has become the recognised instrument for Maori to assert their rights, negotiate power-sharing, bargain for resources and generally advance their cause. It may not – as we'll see in the next chapter – have been the correct tool but it was one that demonstrably worked.

But how much cause for regret should that be? Conditions for Maori today are far better than they were two decades ago. Many problems remain, but the progress has been substantial. Correct tool or not, the Treaty was clearly a useful one.

It would be wrong to assume that the Treaty is about to be cast aside, though. If you're waiting it out in Queensland until New Zealand comes back to its senses and ditches the Treaty and stops bowing and scraping to 'those Maoris', you may be staying put on the Gold Coast for a while yet. It may be, though, that the debate begins to consider what measures Maori might best use from now on to advance their cause. And that's what we'll be exploring in the next chapter.

Chapter Four

20 May 2068

Wellington

The Supreme Court today lifted an injunction that may finally bring relief for beleaguered Pakeha farmers on Queenstown's Hackett reservation from the kiwi plague that has denuded their worm farms. The Court held that in special circumstances kiwi slaughter, prohibited under Article Two of Te Tiriti, might be permitted. 'At the time of the enshrinement of Te Tiriti in the constitution, few people could have predicted that kiwi alone, of all birds, would survive the avian flu, nor that Maori would have proven to have a resistance 80 per cent greater than any other race to the transmutated virus and the global pandemic that ensued,' the Court held.

Minority Pakeha, the Chief Justice noted, though not expressly protected by Te Tiriti from the depredations of avian flu and its consequences, were entitled to expect a reasonable degree of protection from the State. Consequently, they should be permitted to harvest kiwi for export in numbers sufficient to permit their worm farms to recover. The prohibition on harvesting of fern leaves for export as medicinal treatments remained in effect, however. 'The symbol on our flag holds deep spiritual

*significance. The cultural affront entailed in packaging
ferns for commercial use is too controversial a practice to
be contemplated,' she said.*

IF YOU want to know where to apportion the credit for China's
booming economy, you might consider giving some to Deng
Xiaoping. He famously declared that he didn't much care
whether a cat was black or white as long as it caught mice. Thus,
the world's largest communist nation got permission from its
leader to take an altogether more open-market approach to its
economy. Pragmatism can sometimes be a useful way of looking
at the world.

Pragmatism, Andrew Sharp notes, has been a feature of our
negotiation of Treaty issues. He has written that people who
took this point of view were happy to 'fudge' it. We had
arguments, he points out, that didn't seem capable of being
solved: people could not agree on what rights Maori and Pakeha
respectively had, and what was due to them. In the face of
impossible disagreement, the past two decades saw deals,
settlements and arrangements that could be *lived with.*
Pragmatic resolutions, in the face of altogether-too-difficult
philosophical disagreements.

If that's so, is there a better way of going about this? Sharp
says we fail to look at issues in a useful way. Take, he says, the
way the foreshore debate developed:

> You've replaced a common law regime with a statutory one –
> and a statutory one in the end more favourable to Maori than
> the common law one. It's just a statutory regime, which will
> work, substituting for a common law regime which probably
> did nothing. But the problem with doing anything was what
> bedevils our politics – brash symbolism.

That's why, he says, he doesn't like the Treaty much, because it
doesn't mean anything until you get down to details and clarify

your meanings, and once you do, you're in trouble because whatever you do there's going to be disagreement.

> And it's the same with this. It was a debate where meanings were uncontrolled – anything could happen, anything could be said, all of this might seem somehow to be relevant to what was at issue, but none of it was.

He says we New Zealanders do a pretty poor job of isolating, clarifying and writing about precisely what it is we're arguing about. And because we don't analyse and understand those arguments, we don't actually see the consequences of our arguments. He gives the example of the way the debate took shape in the mid-1970s about reparation for past wrongs:

> It was assumed – far too easily, I think – that there was some substance in the argument. There wasn't any substance at all. What there *is*, is an emotional commitment to repairing the past, doing something about it. But the moment you think about that – that justice requires putting back people in the position they would have been in if the wrong hadn't been done, compensating them in such a way that they're now capable of competing in the way that they would have been [able to] – the minute you begin to phrase it specifically in one of those ways or otherwise, then you'll see that *intellectually* the task's totally impossible. You *can't* put people back in the position that they would have been in had the wrong not been done.

Why not? Because, he says, so much has happened since the wrong took place. History could have taken people in so many different directions, depending on what happened next and what happened after that and so on, that we just can't say what position they would have been in today if the wrong had not happened. It would depend on 'external accidents, their own effort, luck, all sorts of stuff like that. If you are thinking about compensation that we could make in the present, it's impossible for those reasons to calculate what that would be'.

And if the parties to the argument don't share the same culture, he says, it's much, much worse. Say you don't agree that what Pakeha did to Maori was wrong. You see it as good, clean conquest or normal fraud or colonisation by a great empire, or whatever. If you don't regard it as wrong, the whole scenario of ill faith, disgust, unwillingness to discuss the thing, starts to occur.

> Now I thought that was the case in the very beginning. It should have been much clearer that there could be no just compensation or no just right or wrong; all there could be was some symbolic recognition that a wrong had been done.

So is there a better way? Well, assume for a moment that it's not possible to agree on any obligations that arise from what happened in the past. If we just ask about a proper distribution of things today, where does that take us?

> I don't think it should matter – this is my personal view – *what* the Treaty says about this. What does matter is this: that a government has got a duty to maintain the peace and prosperity. And if it's to do that, it can't allow a section of the population to fare much worse than any other section of the population. If, in addition, that part of the population suffers because of what happened to it in the past . . . then there are two sets of reasons why a government should attend to the disadvantage of that section of the population.
>
> The first is to bring about the peace and prosperity of the place, and the second is not to let those people be disadvantaged by their past history. There used to be a third argument – the socialist argument roughly, let's just call it the egalitarian argument – that New Zealand is not the kind of place you would want to have huge disparity in power and income and life chances among groups of people. And what you would do is you would find those groups of people who didn't have this power of life chances and you'd give them that power of those life chances. So the government's got to keep peace and prosperity;

it's right that you should help people who are disadvantaged through no fault of their own in the past, and [so] there's the egalitarian argument that you just don't want a lot of people without [those chances].

I've been able to say these things using ordinary European-derived discourse without ever mentioning the Treaty, and I actually think it would be much healthier to proceed in that way, because then we can speak directly.

If you do it this way, he says, it's much better than talking Treaty-wise because you can actually see what's at stake.

I mean the government can say to us: *Why we're doing this is because we're pursuing a biculturalism of fear. We fear that if we don't, then this country won't be so prosperous; that a group of people won't behave so well, there'll be prison problems, hospital problems . . . so out of this fear, we proceed to advantage these people above others.*

And on that argument, so they should.

Or they'd say: *Among all the dispossessed, people stricken with poverty and ill health, there's a certain group that are being more disadvantaged than others simply by facts about the past that give them no choice; they should in particular be helped by government policy.* Or there's a third one, and this is the Brash one, [and] though Brash wouldn't like to admit it, it's a very socialist egalitarian argument: *If anyone's in need they should get what they need – that's what governments are for.* So Brash is straight-down-the-line, old-fashioned social welfare state egalitarianism and the Labour Party has been mostly that, but with a dose of the second – the idea that people couldn't help it because of the past wrongs [and] they should be compensated.

There's a second point to this, he notes: 'What I've talked about doesn't always generate duties – it just tells you what's good to do or what's better, so you balance – which is actually prag-matic. But if you're talking Treaty stuff, it's *duty* that's laid upon the Crown.' And when there's duty then other people have rights, and they can agitate for those rights and demand justice and if necessary kill, because the idea of justice is that if it's not done then you can punish the person who doesn't do it. 'So the Treaty justice discourse is hideously misplaced when you're thinking about distribution.'

> I think New Zealanders' ideology is a very strange mixture of egalitarian liberalism and redneckery. The appeal of the idea of one law for all . . . is extremely powerful. And it's kind of true, it would seem to us. And Brash then put his finger on something which we all believed . . . I mean, what New Zealander *wouldn't* believe that people in need should get stuff before people who don't? And who wouldn't think that there *shouldn't* be special and unwarranted preferential treatment?

He recalls the difficulty which the Labour Government encountered with its *Closing the Gaps* policy: 'The minute it got publicised, it got shut down and they shut it down because it looked ethnically challenging. But I think they also shut it down because it looked socialistic – that's the way I feel. More of a socialistic thing than a racial thing.'

> And I actually think that Brash has played into the hands of the Labour Government, rather, because he's given them permission from the right wing to actually undertake social welfare policies, and I think that lies deep in a lot of old Labour politicians – mind you, so it should – and so I think in the long term it actually destroys National's [position], because what can it do now? It's got nowhere to go. And no overt appeal to racial prejudice will appeal to the polity, because we're actually egalitarian, so you can't do the race thing. And quite clearly, you can't.

If we want to make more sense of this, he argues, we really need to talk about philosophy.

> It strikes me as very alarming that we've allowed our Treaty debate to be taken over by historians. They don't think. Historians tell stories about the past, and they'll often tell

correct ones, but you actually don't learn from the past unless you ask yourself *What principles does the past show me?*

But then the minute you ask yourself *What principles does the past show me?* another question arises: *Are these principles right or not? Should I follow them? There's no obvious reason why I should . . .*

Sharp's contention is that we don't manage to step outside our law and custom and our own history and assess what we're doing philosophically. We're lucky, he says, that what we've contrived to do is actually working – nobody's fighting and governments can negotiate. But let's not kid ourselves that what we've done will stand much intellectual scrutiny: let's be modest and simply recognise that we're lucky that we can get away with it.

We are still very egalitarian in our feelings about distribution, wealth and opportunity, and we remain very anti-intellectual – 'that is to say, we don't like our ideas played out and exposed and shown for what they are, and I think those characteristics in society have both good and bad effects. I think if either of those things changed a lot, *we'd* change'.

So we got it wrong, then? At the very least, it seems, we've used the Treaty for more than it was capable of. But it's done. We are now – as the joke about the tourist in Ireland goes – in the position of asking the farmer how to get to Dublin and being told *If I were going to Dublin I wouldn't be starting from here.* The fact is: we *are* here, the Treaty *does* matter – to *many* interested parties – and whether it was the appropriate tool for every circumstance or not, it carried us to this point.

In the Motunui case, for example, Maori found that you could use the Treaty to stop the majority riding roughshod over your rights. You could go to the Tribunal and point out that your fishing grounds were being trashed by Pakeha authorities and the Treaty gave you the clout you needed to make them back off.

And once a tool works well for you, you tend not to put it away. The Treaty turned out to work in a variety of situations. In fact, what couldn't it do? It sliced, it diced, it julienned. It got Maori leverage in Parliament in the government, in the bureaucracy in the courts, and in the nation's many debates. Once it's delivered you fisheries, Treaty settlements, seats at the table and resources, it's a pretty good bet you'll be using it not as your last resort, but as the weapon of choice.

And it wasn't just Maori who liked what it did. Politicians, bureaucrats and the courts all ended up going along for the ride. It proved to be a very handy tool for analysing and responding to issues. But, as Andrew Sharp points out, the wider public never really got involved in the discussion. And now the bungee cord has come flying back. So if the Treaty *is* being incorrectly used, how do you resolve things in a constructive and pragmatic way?

For starters, you need to factor in that various parties to this debate have very different points of view; so different, in fact, that it's arguable whether you might find any common ground.

You might – and many do – take the view that Treaty rights are what valid law says they are – no more and no less, and that the Treaty relationship of Maori with the Crown is simply what the Crown says it is. The Crown is undeniably in charge and what that theoretically implies is that it can make the Treaty as significant or as immaterial as it likes.

But that's not the only point of view in this debate. There's the Maori constitutional viewpoint which says that the Treaty is everything: a covenant; a founding document that locates power.

And to make things just a little bit more interesting, there's yet another perspective. You also have those people who take the view that their iwi – by virtue of their special attachment to certain land – hold special constitutional standing with respect to that area.

How much common ground can you get out of all that? Is it even worth debating it, or do you just pragmatically let things roll on, developing slowly in the courts, out of sight of energetic debate, and wait to see if society just evolves and coalesces around a position? Or do you try the constitutional stocktaking approach the government has proposed without any conspicuous vigour?

Chris Trotter has a somewhat more lively suggestion. What if you got together a debate on TV that would run not just for an hour or two, but for several days or more? And what if you comprised it according to the population proportions of the country? The idea was born out of a conversation with Andrew Sharp who suggested a citizens' jury – an American idea. He proposed it in a column, discussed it with the people in the Human Rights Commission, who took it to TVNZ. But they 'just didn't have either the will or felt – I imagine – [they] couldn't sustain the expense'.

> It would need to be done for at least a week. And it would need to be put in prime time and it would need to be promoted to the skies. And it would need to be done without advertising. And broadcast for a couple of hours every night over five days.

Oh yes, they'd love that. What's a week of ads here or there? You'd do it with a truly randomised audience, chosen like a jury, probably using the jury lists to do it. And you'd use proper statistical moderation to make sure that it did reflect the composition of the New Zealand population 'because I think it's very important for Pakeha to see how overwhelming their majority is and to see how vulnerable 16 per cent are to 84 per cent'.

> If you see 84 people ganging up on 16 you can see it's not fair.
> You can step back and you can say *I see why they get upset*,
> because every time they put up an idea then 'boom' down comes
> this great majoritarian sledgehammer to crush it.

You'd need five days to get through the initial, shall we say,
passion. 'You would have to have the Jerry Springer security
guards around to pull people apart . . . and then the wiser heads
emerge from the ruck, as it were. To say *Well this isn't getting us
anywhere is it?*'

Don't assume the numbers would imply a Maori defeat, he
says. 'They're still here. Stronger than ever because they haven't
committed themselves to death-or-glory fights in the last ditch.
They are very canny politicians, the Maori.'

Canny or not, the tide that was coming in looks to have
peaked for now. If you liked the direction it was heading, the
best outcome you can probably expect for the immediate future
is the approach taken by the Government to hold the line, act
tough on any apparent anomalies or electorally unpalatable
policy and reassure Maori that their special interests will
continue to be recognised (with the important qualification that
if you're deemed to take a more activist role and you happen to
be working in the public service, you may well feel some heat).

By contrast, the tide could go out some way if a politician
had a mind to try it on: strip out references to the Treaty in
legislation; shut down the Waitangi Tribunal or truncate its
scope; withdraw funding and support for Maori provider
groups in health, education and welfare. What would you get?
Probably not bloodshed, as we've seen, but you would certainly
get disaffection, eroded morale, and an eroded sense of
purpose amongst groups who are doing so much to change the
Maori story.

And *why*? Why would you take such pointless steps to solve

a potential problem that's far more imagined than real? Why would you demoralise people and create unnecessary antagonism just to fix a problem that wasn't really there and replace it with a festering larger one?

I grew up in a New Zealand where you didn't have to look far to find someone who could tell you that Maori were less than able; were inadequate, inclined to failure or lazy. I've spent most of my adult life watching the country become better than that. It doesn't especially trouble me that the way the Treaty was used may not have been, intellectually, the soundest way to go. It would trouble me more if we had failed to do anything. I look – pragmatically – at what was achieved (notwithstanding the mistakes). I look at the contrast between the problems being discussed at the first Hui Taumata in 1984 and the one that was held 21 years later, and I see every reason to feel positive. The talk at the 2005 hui was about education and skills, enterprise and business. It wasn't about grievance, and it wasn't about the past. If you don't like the preoccupation with the Treaty, there was plenty about that gathering to encourage you.

But let's leave the talk to one side: just look at the numbers that came out of the hui:

- In 1983, around 12,500 Maori children were enrolled in early childhood education. In 2003, that number was nearly 34,000.

- In 1986, there were around 3000 Maori tertiary students. In July 2003, 62,574 Maori were enrolled in formal tertiary education. (A disgruntled cynic might say: They're all at Te Wananga o Aotearoa learning golf. Let's see what emerges when the dust settles. The tail often wags the dog in a scandal. It would be surprising if this instance proves to be much different.)

- The tertiary participation rate for Maori in 2003 was 23% compared to 13% for non-Maori.

- In 2003, Maori made up 17% of industry trainees. By comparison, 10% of the employed workforce were Maori.

- Between 1981 and 2001, the number of Maori who were self-employed or employers more than trebled to just over 17,000.

- Maori are exporting at a significantly higher rate than the total New Zealand economy. The Maori economy is estimated to make up 1.4% of the total economy and generates 2.3% of exports.

Unemployment is down to eight per cent and the renaissance has momentum. What class of fool would want to jeopardise that? Whatever ideology or intellectual abstraction you want to apply to this, the cats are catching more mice. A pragmatic politician would be wise to weigh their options carefully as they look further out into this new century.

Chapter Five

PEOPLE LIKE US

14 September 2035

Auckland

Prime Minister Michael Wong today warned Kiwi National Front leader Gordon Hilicone to reconsider his threat to blockade the Auckland Harbour Tunnel. Hilicone's white supremacists seized control of the tunnel during the turmoil of the Mairangi Bay eruption, and have refused to vacate the tunnel until funding is reinstated for the National Front's boarding school for young white ladies. 'We have been patient, but the Front has made its point now, and it should consider returning to the bargaining table,' insisted Wong. 'We are committed to maintaining funding for minorities in this country, but the Front's demands for funding are entirely unrealistic. All four harbour bridges remain gridlocked while the tunnel is closed, and the situation simply cannot continue.'

FEELING GOOD about the value of your Auckland airport shares? No reason why you shouldn't: look how far they've climbed since you bought them. Of course it's helpful to have a quasi-monopoly in your chosen market; just ask the six- and seven-figure salaried folks over at Telecom.

But I digress. The nice chunky profits that are keeping Auckland airport shares on the rise reflect a global trend. More people landed at Auckland in January 2005 than ever before; and across the world, ever more people are on the move. But not everyone is making the trip in an airliner with a choice of 50 movies and a fine selection of wines, we must remember. There's no shortage of people willing to hand over their life savings for the dubious pleasure of being crammed into a container and trucked into Europe. It's the containers with non-human cargo that still constitute the norm, though, and they are moving at greater rates than ever before.

Tourism, fuelled by increasingly affordable airfares, just doesn't stop growing, and trade and migration gather more momentum all the time. We have a global stew on the boil.

If you like the idea of each culture keeping to itself and every country of the world being composed of one predominant race, this is a bad time to be a citizen of the world. I like diversity and variety. I'm optimistic about our capacity to absorb the change that comes with new settlers and new cultures. But I'm aware that not every citizen shares my point of view.

A year or two into the new century, a Howick woman found herself standing in a bank and noticed that the five other people in the queue were of Asian descent. So were the tellers and the bank manager. She began to cry. She wrote a letter to the New Zealand Herald declaring that she felt 'like an alien in my own country'. The Asian invasion, eh? What can we do to stem the inflow of investment, the contribution of new hard-working citizens, the cultural variety that makes our largest city a little more cosmopolitan? What can we do to preserve the fragile cultural toehold of the likely 50 to 60 per cent white population which statistics suggest we'll have two decades from now?

If it's any comfort, we're not alone in this. The same global stew is having some interesting (and contradictory) consequences right across the globe.

Contradiction number one: on the one hand, some people fret about local cultures and national identities being submerged under the weight of American consumerism: *In come the Golden Arches, and the Starbucks, out goes the local café*. But on the other hand, how do you square that with the way so many of us shop from the world bazaar? We're much more free to share and exchange across the world, and we do. We eat Asian food, we watch movies from the Middle East, we read South American literature, we travel, we trade, we learn other languages, and we form relationships with people all around the world.

Globalisation and technology has pressed a kind of fast-forward button on the phenomenon, but there's nothing especially novel about it. It's been going on for centuries. History suggests that the cultures that thrive are the ones that keep changing. They respond to all kinds influences: technology, knowledge, fashion, new ideas. Stand in the middle of New York, or London or Berlin, or nearer to home – Sydney or Melbourne, for example – and you see the process at work. It's fast, it's vibrant, and there's an endless exchange and interaction of different lives.

But you may notice something else. Each of those cities will have great diversity, but to some degree, they'll look alike because each one is an example of a player that's collected the whole set. They are all very diverse, but that fact can make them look quite similar in their greater form.

What seems especially significant is the extent to which these communities cope with this diversity; not in the sense that everything is sweetness and light, and not to suggest that established communities don't give new communities a tough ride, but that over time, they have demonstrated a capacity to absorb and integrate diverse populations – generally to the benefit of the community as a whole.

Consider New York. In *The Island at the Centre of the World*, Russell Shorto demonstrates that it was Amsterdam – the most liberal city in Europe – that became the model for the city that would become, in time, New York. The Amsterdam of the seventeenth century was a pioneer. It absorbed many refugees from a variety of European theatres of war and persecution. It had been the most active of all trading societies. It had been compelled to find a way for many different peoples and cultures to work alongside one another, and it had developed an unusual policy of tolerance and diversity. Its influences, as Shorto tracks them through the early years of Manhattan Island, clearly provided a model for a city that remains today quite strikingly different from the rest of the United States.

Amsterdam also provided a model for accommodating the great waves of people that fuelled the growth of an economic superpower. It was New York that would take in the huddled masses in their millions, at the turn of the twentieth century, and accommodate wave after wave of European migrants. It is New York still where many migrants – Asian, Latino, eastern European – begin their new lives. And as they did in those earlier waves, they change America even as they adapt to its ways.

But what does this mean if you're standing in your bank in Howick blinking away your tears? If you absorb wave after wave of immigrants, does the identity of your country change? Inevitably. But what is it that you're wanting to retain that makes you fret so much? What aspects of life, aside from the colour of the skin of these new people around you – and the language they speak – do you see changing? You can still come home from work each night to see Judy Bailey cocking her head in that reassuring way as she delivers your nightly news. The kids still play in the same playground at your local park. You can still have a picnic at the nearby beach and those damn Asians have stopped cleaning out the shellfish there since the council sorted things out. The fish-and-chip shop around the corner still serves up the same high-cholesterol weekend treat you've always enjoyed. The new owners do a good job of cooking them too. They come from Korea, as it happens.

A sweeping generalisation: Winston Peters seems to garner most of the support for his immigration stance from older people. Perhaps it becomes harder to adjust to change when you've already had a lifetime of doing so. Hekia Parata noticed something of the kind at the world premiere of *Tama Tu* – a film about six Maori Battalion soldiers waiting for night to fall in the wreckage of a ruined Italian home.

> Two Hollywood stars came to it: front page, above the centre line of the *Dominion*, and I was really intrigued that readers of the *Dominion* were flowing in the rest of the week saying: *This is total cultural hijacking, the story was about Tama Tu, there were 30 Maori Battalion men that came from all over New Zealand, yet not a photo of those 80-year-old faces graced our papers. Instead you've got two non-New Zealand Hollywood stars and that tells us we're okay because these two attended it.*
>
> Anyway . . . there was no dialogue in the entire twenty minutes. It's all facial expressions and it is extremely cultural. I may be being unfair, but in the theatre watching it, I was really intrigued that younger New Zealanders, all friends of the twenty producers and directors and what not, hooted with laughter over the start, as did all the Maori. Much older Pakeha New Zealanders were not sure what the joke was and it was really interesting to see that younger Pakeha New Zealanders get it. There wasn't that pained self-consciousness of trying to understand what the Maoris were saying. They got it. They were into it. They're all friends together. But these older ones . . .

If coping with this issue is in fact a phenomenon of age, then an older person has quite an amount to cope with. There's a good argument you can make that national identity itself is becoming less significant. We're all citizens of the world – or at least those of us with the money to use technology like the Internet and those of us who can travel.

That means we have the capacity to form our own communities that have little to do with national identity. If you're a scientist, you may join communities with scientists of similar interest. A sports fan or music fan may form close connections with people elsewhere in the world who have the same posters on their walls. Politics, business, travel all give people reason to make connections across the world, and they do. They form new communities, in the way people have always done. The difference today is that you can create one that crosses a dozen time zones.

That's not to say that you won't also be inclined to share some kind of national identity. The language you speak, the place where you were born, the problems you've faced and the experiences you've been through all bond you to your fellow citizens to some degree. But in the decades ahead, those bonds will probably become looser. Being a New Zealander doesn't mean you won't also be other things, and some of those other identities may at times have more significance to you.

Immigration, then, should surely not be anything to bother us – should it? Is our way of life really in danger? Senior lecturer in Communications at AUT Wayne Hope has some reservations. He believes the argument is not whether we should have immigration or not, or whether we've got too much immigration or too many immigrants. The argument is where should they come from and what should the demographic mix of New Zealand be? If we are going to have cultural priorities with regard to immigration, he would rather they be more biased toward the South and South-West Pacific than towards South-East Asia:

> I'm not saying we only want Pacific Islanders and not the Chinese diaspora, but I think there is a lack of balance because what is happening in Auckland is that you've got a higher Asian and Chinese population than a Polynesian population and they came in so quickly that there's been no integration or absorption; and why are they here?
>
> Well partly it's because schools just want their students' money; successive governments have thought that a points system of immigration would kick-start our economy; and there's all these short-term reasons for having that pattern of immigration but no long-term planning about it, and it's creating a situation where the demographic mix of New Zealand doesn't reflect where we live. I think there's a real problem there.

New Zealand's base population, he points out, is very small, as the Maori population was in the nineteenth century when it was swamped by white colonists. 'I'm not saying it's happening again, but in a funny way we're revisiting similar demographic issues and the point about that is we are a very young country.' He contrasts that with the situation of a large, long-established place like Barcelona:

> It's just a polyglot place – people from all over Europe, all over Northern Africa, people from the Caribbean – just piles of people with all sorts of ethnicities and cultures. But the point about Spain is that it is a very, very old country with long traditions which are a hybrid of different cultures – Islam, Catholicism, Judaism and all the rest of it. So when you get all those different influences over time it builds up a sediment – a long history. An older country can absorb shifts in demography but a really young country like New Zealand – that's a real problem and you have to be very careful.

The Maori, Hope argues, had their cultural traditions swamped by new immigrants and the history of the country became the history of those who came last. He sees a similar threat by today's immigrants to our nation's identity and culture.

> I'm already running into difficulties teaching, because you're so reliant on money from full fee-paying overseas students. They don't care about learning about New Zealand – that's not what they're here for and yet [if you have] any sense of courtesy that's what you do isn't it? You learn about the country you go to . . .
>
> No, [for them] it's about getting their degree. There is a danger that growing numbers of people living within New Zealand have no real interest where they've come from in the past – and I'm not saying it's the same for all immigrants, but I think it's a problem if you let your demography get out of kilter.

He's noticed around Auckland – places like Mt Roskill and Dominion Road – that whereas there used to be more of a public Polynesian culture, now it's tipped all the other way. 'You get the distinct impression that all the Polynesians are getting pushed out to Manurewa, basically, and I don't think that's good – I really don't.'

> I tell you what I did notice, just anecdotally – the last Pasifika Festival I went to, I hardly saw any Asian people there – that's interesting isn't it? There is some cultural fragmentation occurring because of the changing – because of the rapid changes in our demographics which I think are worth reflecting on.

Could these changes be a threat to the indigenous culture? Where does Maori identity and culture fit in this global mix? Hekia Parata points out that she can practise being Ngati Porou, while also being very bicultural, while at the same time being an internationalist. 'I don't see the need to trade any of those off at all,' she says, and adds that she thoroughly enjoys the way the country is fusing its Maori, Pacific, Asian and Pakeha identities, but doesn't see that we therefore have to embrace that as the one-defined-way of New Zealand life.

It offers a rich vein to explore for New Zealand, she says, but that doesn't mean it's the one true way. It may influence how she wants to dress and the jewellery she wears, and the art she enjoys, and the food she might want to eat, 'but that doesn't mean I don't want to participate in Ngati Porou rituals around tangihanga that aren't fused with anybody'.

And it doesn't mean, she adds, that when she travels internationally she won't choose to describe herself simply as a middle-class New Zealander. 'This is the kind of experience we have in my country. They're not either/ors, they are just and/and.'

> I think it is important that we have Maori-speaking Maori and that we create opportunities for New Zealanders of any culture to speak Maori, but unless we have that fundamental pool of people speaking Maori that then lends its language, allegories and whatnot to poetry and music and art, then we don't have a well from which we can continue to draw.

She thinks it matters that we honour the original agreement to settle in this country together by protecting the wellspring for the culture. And, she says, it has to adapt to contemporary needs:

> You get the naysayers saying: *Oh well, what allows Maori to talk about having the opportunity to be involved in broadcasting, because there weren't radio waves in 1840.* No there weren't, but there weren't tractors either and we're not stopping Massey-Ferguson ploughing up the farms of pioneer descendants.

It's just such an unhelpful kind of debate to get into, she thinks. 'Yes, there absolutely has to be protection of indigenous culture in New Zealand, and that principle of indigenity has to be balanced alongside all the other principles of economic wellbeing and social justice, and so forth in order [for us to] have the strong and positive future that we do have as a nation.'

If you consider that the culture ought to be protected and preserved, how do you go about it? With the Treaty? Andrew Sharp points out that many countries manage to do so without reference to any Treaty. 'Why wouldn't you allow, and at times, help, people [to] preserve things about their culture? Why do you need a treaty for that?' he asks.

> If you are brought up in a minority culture or a threatened culture, which is getting thinner or dying out, your choices are constricted. So the idea is that when there is a societal culture – that is to say, a culture that'll give you a whole range of options that will enable you to lead a decent life – then those cultures should be preserved for the sake of autonomy.
>
> So if you want to be able to live as Maori – and why shouldn't you? – then what they'll need is their culture preserved. Without that, they can't make choices as Maori. That's the liberal argument. What other arguments are there? Well, it's hard to think what other arguments there are, and that's why the Treaty cuts in to say something like *We can't think of any argument why Maori culture should be preserved except that it's a taonga which was promised us under Article Two of the Treaty.* Now that *can't* be right. Can it? It's just so thin.
>
> And again, it makes things a matter of duty, you know, 'the crown *must* [act in a certain way]' and so on, whereas when it gets to the courts and the Privy Council, it doesn't become like that, it becomes a duty to provide [things]. These things can't be matters of duties, they've got to be matters of balance. And Maori have got to say to themselves, *Well: how much of this do I want, and how much of that, and how am I going to do it?* And if you talk to Maori – especially Maori trust boards and corporations – they're always steering some preservation or a change in the culture and so on.
>
> I find it very hard to think that many Maori would want a static unchanging society where what was preserved was just what was there before.

Indeed. And there are those who wonder whether Maori are looking in the wrong direction by seeking to preserve a particular way of life. This is a tune some people hesitate to whistle out loud. One academic I interviewed on this subject preferred to comment anonymously:

> I think the Maori are catching themselves in an impossible situation. I mean, there is Tariana Turia waving the flag of Maori culture, riding around in a car and wearing Western dress and living in hotels and so on. If she's really sincere, she'd be running around in grass skirts and going barefoot – not even horse riding is appropriate. Everybody nowadays says we want to co-operate, we want to preserve indigenous culture, we don't want to disadvantage or marginalise anybody – but indigenous Maori culture is incompatible with modern Western money-based markets and so on.

Western culture, he argues, is a kind of 'non-culture' – it's a dropping-away of old cultures. If you want to live in the modern, developed world it's necessary that you adopt the whole Western, rational, secular world-view. You rely on scientific inquiry and method, and not on spirituality and cultural norms that can impede rational thought. If you really want to revivify or protect indigenous Maori culture, how can you drive around in planes, or have a Maori TV station – it's not part of the indigenous culture. By trying to do two things at once, you're dismantling the culture you profess to want to preserve. You want to keep in touch with your indigenous values and yet at the same time you ditch them because they stand in the way of your TV and your life insurance and your private property, et cetera.

> It's a Siberian dilemma situation actually. The Siberian dilemma is you go fishing in Siberia, and the ice breaks and you fall in – you've got exactly twenty seconds to decide whether you want to die by drowning or climbing out and freezing to death before you can dry yourself.

> Adam Smith in *The Wealth of Nations* was absolutely outspoken about this. He said, *Look, you can't have it both ways. If you keep your cultural taboos and beliefs, they stop your mobility and above all you've got to be mobile – to break up your homestead and go where there're jobs offering.*

Historian Bill Oliver begs to differ. He thinks there is a great richness to having more than one cultural affiliation:

> In my own case, my parentage, not just my ancestry, is Cornish, and I take great pleasure in having that affinity, which is somewhat weaker than the Welsh or the Irish or the Scottish, but I think the whole trend of history runs contrary to [the view that there's this Western arc that everyone should join].

To give the argument its due, he says, Maori of today are an enormous distance from the Maori of 1840, 'and though Pita Sharples may dress up in a strange gown . . . there is an element of the cosmetic and the antiquarian about it'.

> I felt this most strongly once when I started looking at the Ngata-inspired meeting houses on the east coast. They are beautiful but they were a deliberate revival of a disappeared style.

He describes a house that was built to receive Te Kooti:

> It was a beautiful house when it was built, a great whare, [but] it has now been rather overrestored by Maori persons with paint brushes. It's a painted house, one of the great . . . painted houses and I saw it before it was restored and it was magic. I think it still is great, but it was magical in those days. There's hardly any carving, the house went up in a hurry. And they painted the interior to some extent traditionally, but these panels between the tukutuku, wood panels: a beautiful Maori woman in a dress, there's flowers, there's a missionary with a book in his hand, there's a settler with an axe to the tree, there's even – because a racecourse is nearby – a racehorse and a jockey clearing a hurdle.

It's clear enough that Maori have adapted their traditional culture. It's not been preserved in aspic. But neither has the culture been cast off, and the renaissance of the past generation has made it a much more noticeable aspect of New Zealand life. Is that a potential handicap? By failing to embrace Western culture exclusively, is anyone impeded? Hekia Parata thinks not. She mentions the Oscar-nominated short film *Two Cars, One Night* about three Maori children sitting in cars outside a pub waiting for their parents, and sees a number of signs of hope.

> [Firstly] we're actually getting a film made by Maori. One of the things Cliff Curtis as producer said that night to a packed Embassy Theatre was: *It's important for us as Maori to tell Maori stories about ourselves to ourselves so that we can present ourselves to New Zealand and to the world.* He said, *I'm usually cast as a Mexican bandit, or whatever, in Hollywood.* So it's really important that we are able to tell Maori stories in New Zealand, in the natural location for them. That makes us accessible. I'm really hopeful about that. And music now, and books and poetry and dance, these are all things that celebrate that cultural advantage.

She sees a whole philosophy of positivism 'and it's not apologist. New Zealanders relate to it. It's a Maori story told by Maori, but lots of young Pakeha New Zealanders are just so gung-ho about it and so at-home [with it]. They didn't think it was a big deal. It's natural'.

She offers the Pasifika fashion show as another example of a distinctive cultural style emerging here. All the designers had used symbols of the Pacific and New Zealand in their clothes, but what interested her especially was that 'TV1 thought it was good enough to be on prime-time television', and secondly that it was a fusion – 'it was Maori, Pacific, Asian, Pakeha New Zealand'. Each line had music to suit:

. . . so they had that Samoan tenor who is now making it big in the world, he sang *Ave Maria* to the bridal display, and then they had some hip hop PI group doing urban male. It was just such a combination of who we're becoming. That was fabulous. We have got this amazing flowering of the small Pacific Island states. We've now got this strong Asian dimension coming in. There is potential for this fusion to swirl above that, but it does rely, I think, on ensuring that those foundation cultures are strong in their sense of who they are so that they can be participants in what we are becoming.

Margaret Mutu takes issue with the notion that Maori need to shrug off culture and join the prevailing Western 'non-culture'. There's an assumption she encounters with bureaucrats that 'what is the Pakeha world is the norm and everything else shall be measured beside it, according to that norm'. She was brought up in both cultures. 'Each of them has their quite distinct and different ways of seeing the world.' To say that only you have a culture and Pakeha don't is, she says, completely absurd. But the Pakeha system, she says, assumes it's always right and always superior.

> I've often had to say to officials, *You know, you assume that your way is the right way, but in actual fact your way is only one way of many others and this is perhaps one of the fundamental problems you have in this.*
>
> It's the biggest problem we have when people come into our area, and the engineers will tell you this is a planning process. You go to the council, the council has its hearings, and it only wants to hear from the engineers, the planners, the landscape architects and those sorts of people, because they are the people who know.
>
> And we say, *well, hang on a minute, they only know a snapshot of what they see now. They have no knowledge at all of the history or the background or the hundreds of years of experience of this.*
>
> What we've said to them, time and time again is, *You do*

*yourselves a huge disservice by not looking at all of the knowledge
that is held. You only want to look at the knowledge that you know
as your [scientific] approach – the facts as you define them within
your cultural norms. In actual fact, your cultural norms are blind to
a lot of areas that we know a lot about.*

She guesses that that sends out conflicting messages. 'We're
always happy to listen to what the engineer says and what
the architect says and this one and that one.' But there's no
reciprocation.

We say to them, *In actual fact, that river that's down there, it
wanders all over the place, so if you're going to do something down
there do you realise that that river could have moved half a kilometre
in ten years' time?* And they go, *No, no, no, that can't possibly
happen, da, da, da.* We're telling them it *will.* And they don't want
to know. Of course we can't measure it according to their tools
that they use and we say to them, *But your tools are inadequate.
You don't know what you're talking about.* So we have these huge
arguments – and guess what, they don't listen to us. And then
ten years later, when the sewage pond is not working, we go,
We told you so . . .

That's what we see as so hugely destructive for the country.
These people came in, they deforested the whole country, and
then [they] wonder why they have landslides. There's all this
sort of stuff: the floods, the massive floods we've been having,
you've got to look at land management and why you do it. I
mean Maoridom have been saying for donkey's years, *Do this,
or you'll pay.* Or what we've been saying is, *Don't do it!*

I often look at them, and this is how I perceive these people
– they're children, they're given a bag of lollies and they think
they can just do anything with it. Well, you know, too many bags
of lollies and they're gonna end up being sick. That is what is
happening. And over here you've got the people who gave them
the bag of lollies saying, *no, no, no, just be careful now, we'll help
you deal with that bag of lollies in a way that won't hurt you.* But
they won't, they grab the whole bag of lollies, take the whole

bloody lot, and then you can't get near them. What I often feel
is, give these people another couple of hundred years and maybe
they'll learn.

Anthropology, she notes, is what her Maori Studies department
grew out of, and it is still very much occupied with defining
other people's cultures in terms of Western culture. 'We have
often said to them, *Why don't you study your own culture?* Some
of them do. Some of them study the local cricket club; but an
overall study of the anthropology of Pakeha rule – very rare for
you to get it, they'd rather study other people's cultures.'

For all the enmity and all the bigotry, all the intolerance and
all the bloody-mindedness, all the bleeding-heart woolliness,
we've managed to absorb a good deal of cultural change in a
generation. There's enough intolerance around to tell you that
we're not all good at blending – but really, isn't that what
Queensland is for?

The world has a long and bloody record of conflict, but for
the most part, we've taken the fighting outside and many thousands of miles from here. There's no great reason to suppose
things should be very much different this century.

HAVE YOUR SAY

A betting market can be a kind of continuous popular referendum. So what would happen if you had a betting market on aspects of New Zealand's future? Why not open one and find out? This book has a companion website which offers you the chance to place your bets on where we're going.

Go to www.optimisticpredictions.com and you will get an imaginary $100 to wager on each of the fifteen predictions about New Zealand's future. As soon as you place your bet, the market is updated, and the new odds are displayed.

The market offers six predictions based upon this section of the book:

- The Treaty of Waitangi declared null and void.

- Separate Maori House of Parliament established.

- New Zealand becomes a republic.

- National wins the 2005 election, and forms a coalition with the Maori Party.

- Preferential treatment makes Maori the richest citizens on the planet.

- Guardianship of foreshore granted to iwi on all coastline north of Christchurch. Access by non-iwi prohibited.

To place your bet, go to www.optimisticpredictions.com

Famine

Chapter Six

26 January 2055

Hamilton

New Zealand's last remaining productive farm has been sold. The 100-hectare Waikato property was bought for 25 million yuan by the Beijing Tourist Board, and is expected to be converted into a holiday resort. The vendor, Peter Signal, said he felt little regret at bringing an era to a close. 'Farming's shot. I knew the writing was on the wall when Fonterra diversified into hybrid fuels back in 2030. My grandfather talks about the good old days they used to have, but your dollar was only worth 90 US cents back then. At $2.50, you just get creamed by the Brazilians and the Romanians.' Signal said he and his wife would probably be leaving the country. 'Both our kids are working in Singapore. There's not much to keep us here.'

SOME TIME around the mid-1990s, I found myself one evening in tie and suit, name tag clipped to the jacket pocket, at an awards ceremony in the Northern Club. These things always have a little more cachet if you can wheel out a Minister of the Crown, it seems, and on this particular evening the Government's IT visionary and much-acclaimed stand-up act

Maurice Williamson was doing the honours. He was a little short on jokes, but he had a really good disappearing trick to show us. He pulled a ten-dollar note from his wallet and declared to us in his best primary-school show-and-tell fashion: *Five years from today, you won't be using any of these. It'll all be electronic. That's how fast things are changing.* You don't say, Maurice. Ten years on, it's starting to look as though someone at the Reserve Bank forgot to send out the memo.

Oh, but it's easy to scoff. The bolder the prediction, the greater the risk of getting it wrong. Even your very short-term predictions can be tricky. Would you be game to predict what the New Zealand dollar will be doing next month? No? What if you were a highly skilled economist? The BNZ's chief economist, Tony Alexander, was refreshingly candid about this in a 2004 edition of his weekly newsletter. An eight-year analysis of the economists' picks was conclusive: 'Exchange rate forecasting is a waste of time.' He reported that they had only been right – looking ahead on a monthly basis – four times in the previous eight years. 'That's a 4.3% success rate. We are wrong 95.7% of the time – about what you would expect from a monkey tossing a coin.'

Share market then? Richard Flinn of ASB Bank Investments offered a not dissimilar point of view in an article in *Financial Alert*. His answer to two of the questions most often asked in investing: *What do you think the market is going to do in the next month? Or year?* was equally refreshing in its candour: 'We don't have the foggiest idea.'

In the longer run, though, it's a different matter. He professed to be confident that, ten years on, the share market would be 'up from where it is today'. In the short term, the share market is pretty random. Speculators dominate. Over time, though, the investors dominate. Businesses grow over time, the market 'weighs' them accurately, and share prices rise. That's not to say that markets will rise inevitably, but if they don't, it will be for a more fundamental reason: 'the end of capitalism as we know it'.

And that's the cue for a relatively reassuring start to an exploration of the question: *Are we in danger of becoming some kind of banana republic?* In 2004, Don Brash offered a warning in the *Australian Financial Review* that New Zealand risked becoming 'just another Pacific Island state', if we didn't do something to deal with the widening income gap between the two countries. And out in the blogosphere, you'll find people making gloomy noises. Some of the present government's more trenchant critics offer the various predictions that we'll have to be absorbed into Australia because we've squandered every opportunity to invest in any kind of economic future, that the government is taxing the country out of viability, and that all the talent is packing up and moving.

Well, what are the odds? Let's begin by taking the very broadest view. How bad can things get? Can you run the train off the tracks and never get it back on? People sometimes make the comparison with Argentina: a prosperous country, comparable to ours in a number of ways, with a comparable standard of living, until it came completely unstuck. Can you go so far – as they say has happened to Argentina – that you're gone for good? Tim Hazledine is a professor in economics at Auckland University. He notes that Argentina is a name people often suggest, but more significantly, he points out, it seems to be the only one they can come up with. In the 1920s, he agrees, it was as rich as Australia and is now 'almost a basket case'. He suspects the blame can be pinned on its dictatorship, and he wonders if we look at the wrong issue when we ask about the relative performance of our economy to others:

New Zealand hasn't slipped back in that sense. It hasn't declined absolutely. It's been caught up with by a lot of countries, but that's not necessarily a bad thing. And good for them, I'd say. I'd stop publishing these growth leagues . . . don't worry about it, just look at the fundamentals as an economy: look at the sustainability, its use of income, are we running it well?, could we run it better?

New Zealand Business Roundtable Executive Director Roger Kerr disputes the interpretation some people have been making of the league table numbers. At the Knowledge Wave exercise, he complains, people were 'rehearsing the old litany of New Zealand's relative decline in living standards. That is long since untrue'. Practically every country you can think of now, bar the North Koreas and the Cubas, he says, has moved to a more open-market direction. He was always confident that New Zealand would get major gains from doing that. The framework of reform that had been established by the early 1990s 'is very much intact'.

Look at the growth, he says. If you look at 1993 through to 1996, we were averaging four per cent growth; we got up to five and six per cent at one point, then the Asian crisis skewed the picture for a year or two; but now, once again, it's 'basically motoring on through'. And although the present administration has made 'a really small number of positive steps' and we've had 'a much larger number of backward steps' he sees none of them to be 'in any sense cataclysmic'.

This is a much better economy. Much more flexible. It copes with the ups and downs of the rest of the world. You're going to carry on growing at three per cent or something like that on average [with] budget estimates of 1.5 per cent labour productivity growth – and that's the key underlying thing to think about, because that is pretty much your long-term per capita growth rate. So don't start arguing that the sky's going to fall in.

It ain't. The proper argument is that this is as good as it gets under the present set of policies. It ain't gonna get any better. The Government's notion of getting New Zealand back up into the top half of the OECD by getting an acceleration of the growth rate that we're on at the moment: that three per cent is just not going to happen. And if we ever get serious about that, we've got to go back to basically the recipes that got us the gains in the first place. Because they're still the most relevant recipes and there's still plenty of things that can be done.

So he is 'very allergic to anybody who wants to paint a doom-and-gloom scenario'. He doesn't envisage us becoming a Fiji: 'I don't see the remotest possibility of that happening.' But there's a flip side to that. Neither does he foresee 'the remotest possibility' of us being an Ireland or a Singapore.

Kerr says there's absolutely no reason why – 'if we used our wits' – we couldn't be right back at the very top. 'I think we've learned a lot. I don't think the country's at any risk of going back into fortress New Zealand. However, our politics have not been great. We have done what I regard as the good things in fits and starts, and it's an ongoing battle to hold that.' He thinks, looking back some years from now, we may come to see the Helen Clark government as the one that actually entrenched the post-1984 economic changes as the new orthodoxy.

There were probably some people who thought, *Okay, with this final change of government we're going to turn the clock back on a lot of things.* I think the big thing about New Zealand politics, looking at it over twenty years, is that twenty years ago bloody near all our parties were Alliance parties – and I'm meaning now Alliance parties of the Laila Harre sort – that got wiped out at the last election . . . So I'm really confident that we've got ourselves up to a much better level which is robust. But countries can go to sleep again very easily, and in piece-meal fashion they can easily start to make mistakes, which over periods of time start to accumulate again. The Muldoon

> Government and all its predecessors didn't deliberately run the
> country into the ground. They just kind of responded to interest
> group pressures and dumb ideas that were in the ether . . .

And that's how the frog slowly boils. So Kerr gives us a qualified
vote of confidence. Economically, 'there's absolutely no reason
why we couldn't be a standout'. Politically – we'll have to wait
and see. He thinks we're likely to be a pretty successful kind of
country. In today's open world there are a lot more checks and
balances on governments whether they like it or not. 'Financial
market indicators, immigration movements, and things of that
sort.' He thinks those are what will anchor New Zealand to a
much greater degree. 'But if we are solely to rely on those kinds
of things as external governors of some description, if you like,
I don't think we'll be standout.'

> We have to do many more hard yards ourselves and keep on
> doing them. The stories of success are about tough-mindedness
> in good times and bad. You know, to keep on avoiding traps,
> welfare traps, and that kind of thing.

Hands off, then? If you have boundless faith in the invisible
hand, you'll probably follow such a prescription with enthusiasm. The question is, assuming you're confident that you can
expect such an approach to deliver what you want, what proportion of your fellow voters are likely to share your point of
view? In the early days of the revolution, any number of people
were professing their enthusiasm for the invisible hand,
although as some of the excesses of those days have became
clearer in retrospect, a more accurate reading might be that a
fair proportion were confusing the invisible hand with the five-
finger discount.

The incumbent administration, it seems, would certainly
like to believe in the possibilities of a more hands-on *third way*,

and would like to think that intelligent intervention at the appropriate moments can yield good results. They'll no doubt argue that they've stewarded the economy in a way that proves their point. Sceptics will say that they had the best wind at their back a government could ever ask for. If it's true that governments tend to get turfed out when the economy's been bad and they wear the blame for it, they don't have too much to fret about. On the present numbers for growth, inflation, employment, and government accounts, they're probably going to be staying right where they are on the Treasury Benches in the next election. If it weren't for the fairly severe balance of payments situation, things couldn't be looking peachier.

But look at that dollar go. Nearly 75 cents against the US at the time of writing. And look at that hedging running out. Will things still be looking good by election time when the farmers' incomes are coming back down and more exporters have laid-off staff?

Financial journalist Rod Oram notes that the exchange rate today is as high as it was in 1997. 'And back in 1997 and 1998, when the dollar was this high, people were screaming for mercy at 65 US cents to the dollar.' Between 1998 and 1999, he says, 25 per cent of our exporters went to the wall. 'The population of exporters fell from about 12,000 to 9000 . . . and it was a shambles. Today the exchange rate is as high and you don't hear people screaming. It's hard, but people are not screaming for mercy.' Yes, he says, people have been hedging, which has blunted the pain, 'however, it is also correct here that quite a few companies are just smarter, and this is the important thing, not just by being more efficient, and therefore they've taken costs out of the business, but they are actually being more sophisticated and they're able to charge more'. He cautions that with the world economy growing in 2003 by just over five per cent – the fastest growth in a couple of decades – things have been helped along. But even allowing for that, there seems to be more resilience in our economy.

But what about the longer sweep of time? How do we look in broad terms? He suspects that those countries that manage to do well over the long term, and who manage to get through the highs and lows and the changes, probably have some advantages in terms of their location and their resources. You tend to find quite a high level of social cohesion, some shared values, and a determination to move on together. But perhaps most significantly: 'they are also *learning* countries, they sort of say, *This is happening over here, so we will go this way*'. By contrast, you will get people, communities, whole countries, who will be – deliberately or unconsciously – blind to what's going on around them. They don't see that the world's changing and they don't adapt, 'or if they do see it, they react very negatively and very defensively'. Something in the national psyche drives that, he suspects, offering the example of China. Three hundred years ago it accounted for 40 per cent of the world's economy and by 1960 it was down to about one per cent. And it's now heading back up again.

Attitude matters, then. And he warns that we need to be careful in New Zealand not to fool ourselves by assuming we're more favoured than we really are.

> I'm guilty of saying this myself: *This is an amazing land, fantastic climate, it's very temperate, this is a great place to grow things*. Well, no, actually. Rains fail, we didn't really crack agriculture until we understood fertiliser and top-dressing. And our farms have always been very efficient but that's through a lot of hard work and ingenuity, and what concerns me looking ahead is that we are still primary and commodity producers from those resources to a very large extent and we will face very significant

– [and are] already facing, very, very significant – competition from areas that are flat, fertile and with steady rain. The obvious ones are places like Brazil. The topsoil in parts of western Brazil is nine metres thick, and it rains like clockwork and it's as flat as this table and those are becoming amazingly powerful agricultural areas.

Oram thinks we can't be 'the least bit complacent' and sees us running the real risk of simply surfing the wave of prosperous commodity business for the next 'I don't know, five, eight, ten years or so. Partly because of China.' And then suddenly the party could be over and we might not have done enough to diversify and grow. He sees 'amazing opportunities out there in the world' for New Zealand. Take your pick from a vast range of niche possibilities, he says, offering the example of a Glen Eden business making photograph albums that cost thousands of dollars a piece for high-end photographers around the world, but says you don't need to be the least bit prescriptive about it. It doesn't matter. 'Only the unifying, common characteristics matter.' In this view of New Zealand, he suggests, we end up with a bunch of 'marvellously adaptive, creative, fleet of foot' pretty small businesses. And you need another layer above that.

> We need some big businesses because some things, like running an airline, have to be big. Also, it's really important to have some complex organisations because you learn management skills and governance skills there that are more difficult and compli-cated than a small business, but you can then apply quite widely.
> Look, I think the world's always going to be very tough. I am much more interested in resilience, the ability to adapt and sur-vive – survive's a terrible word – *thrive*. Thrive rather than survive. And these [businesses] could be a billion or two New Zealand dollars of revenue a year, which is quite small by international standards, but that starts to feel like a fairly big organisation with quite complicated international operations so we understand how to deal with that complexity. We are getting quite good at

growing companies up to sort of, $50- to $75 million. We are
finding it very hard to grow them to ten times that.

In economies like – say – Germany, Switzerland or Italy, you
have immensely strong, small and medium-sized, typically
privately owned, most typically family-owned, businesses that
have kept growing through a number of generations and are
very international. 'That's the sort of core of companies you are
looking at. And it needs to be a fair chunk of the economy, but
we don't all need to be like that.'

Are more people understanding how to do that? 'Absolutely',
although he's frustrated that the evidence is mainly anecdotal.
He cites Jenny Morel's company, Morel and Co, and then their
venture capital business, No 8 Ventures, holding two confer-
ences in the past two winters, with a 'very interesting bunch of
people invited'.

> Typically relatively high technology, youngish companies
> growing fast, not all companies that No 8's invested in, so it's
> not just a family affair. And I suppose there were about 150 or
> so there, and last year was a marvellous event because it's the
> first time I have been in a group of people like that where there
> was real knowledge about doing these things overseas, and it
> was really exciting. It wasn't like, *Oh God, how do we do that?* It
> was like, *We do this, you do that* ... and it was this amazing
> discussion. And I thought, well, that's a very significant step
> forward, these are people who have got real experience out
> there and this is new, this is new.
>
> On the one hand I am hugely encouraged and I'm very
> encouraging about it, but then I am sort of saying: this is
> absolutely fantastic – but on a scale of one to ten, we're one and
> a half. Don't despair, but let's just try to get to three as quick as
> we can. Shoot for five.

Looking back, though, he judges that something has significantly changed, potentially for the better, in the attitude here.

When he arrived in 1997, New Zealand was 'a bit of a shock in a number of ways'.

> I rapidly came to the conclusion that there was quite a large number of very unhealthy corporate situations, of strategies that were bonkers and not being addressed. Telecom was one. Fletcher Challenge was another. Brierley Investments. Air New Zealand. It just went on and on. And remarkably also, there was still some residual crap floating around even all the way back from the share-market crash and the aftermath of that, and then the world recession at the beginning of the nineties. All that sort of stuff was still working through. And so not only were there some hugely wrong, massively wrong, corporate situations – I mean big ones – but secondly, it was clear there were some economic issues that just weren't being dealt with and there was no discussion [about this].
>
> I think 1998 was a really important year. It was a very tough year. Because you had the Asian crisis and we got very, very pessimistic as a country. But I think out of that pessimism some people started to do stuff positively. I've had that conversation with lots of people who also think that late 1998, early 1999 there was a change and we can't figure out why. It wasn't as though there was some great catalyst. It wasn't as though somebody had flicked a switch. It was like some people just sort of went, *Shit, let's get on with this*. I think the country's been moving in a very interesting direction since, I really do.

The first decade or so of economic reforms, Oram argues, sorted out the playing field in New Zealand and made us a pretty sensible economy, 'but it did nothing to sort out the players in terms of their sophistication and all the rest'.

> Now you could take the optimistic view that, *Well, they'll get there eventually*, but they weren't and it doesn't help when the National Government in the mid-nineties decided that, for example, *If skill training is important and worthwhile to a company, they will do it because they will get economic benefit from it, so we the Government will stand back*. So we got to the point in June

1995 that there were only 18,000 people in the whole country engaged in some formal on-the-job skill training, apprenticeships or whatever. Because if you were a mug as an employer and trained people, I'm the smart employer and I'll come along and hire them afterwards, *Thank you very much. Very nice of you to do that for me.* And we wonder why we've got a skill shortage today.

The government through the 1990s was pretty much inert, he judges. 'It seemed to me it was still convinced government didn't have a role other than not to do anything, that was the first thing, so it didn't want to do anything. It didn't know what to do, other than to do nothing, so that's sort of the macro-component.'

But then the micro-component was Bolger and colleagues were just making a complete hash of the first MMP [government] and just so totally consumed by trying to make MMP work. Then there was the Shipley government and there were a few people in there who were trying to break through, and Max Bradford bravely tried . . . and a) there was no support or traction in Cabinet and b) it was fairly heretical kind of stuff. Given those constraints, and it got very close to the election, it was a brave, vague articulation of something different.

Now we've got a government that is politically astute, handles MMP well, they've got good political skills, competent managers, and their policies – some of their policies – are good; same with any government, some are good, some are dreadful, some are okay patched up a bit.

By contrast, he says, when you talk to Don Brash the stories he tells are of his time as Reserve Bank governor, which has shaped his view of the economy but which leaves little for him to say about today's economy. Oram sees the Brashian view as being 'government shouldn't be involved. Keep it simple, step back, and enterprise will flourish. I want a playing field that's simple'.

Journalist and commentator Russell Brown was reporting on much of the information technology revolution through the 1990s, and he watched an international contrast between the purist New Zealand approach and more interventionist Canadian one. Their telecommunications industry, he recalls, was handled all wrong, according to the purists. They did 'all these wonderful politically incorrect things that we've long been advised in New Zealand were utterly the wrong thing to do and wouldn't work'.

> They regulated prices, they sheltered the cable industry till it got on its feet, they picked winners. And the way they regulated prices was quite interesting. They regulated them on the basis of capital expenditure, so if the telecommunications companies wanted to make more money, they had to build out, and they ended up with a surplus of fibre in the ground – but a surplus of fibre in the ground is probably one of the better kinds of surpluses you can actually have!
>
> And also – rather than leaving the public sector to the market – they decided that municipal buildings, universities, schools and hospitals could be made anchor tenants of new fibre networks; so-called 'mush networks' they ended up being called. And they loaned the money to do it. Of course, once you had those organisations there as guaranteed customers for the fibre, all of a sudden it became much more practical for everyone else to jump in there.
>
> So they did all these things you're not supposed to do and that we didn't do here and they've got the third-best broadband penetration in the world – pricing's *great*. And we sat here with Maurice Williamson declaring memorably, *How can you do better than the best?* – referring to our regulatory environment. And it *didn't work*.

In general, Brown argues, it's smartest to leave markets to make their own decisions, but sometimes – particularly with infra-structure issues – there is a point at which you can prod them, and you get a much better result. He cites what the government's done with Project Probe – 'it's like a very scaled-down version of mush networks'.

They decided they wanted all the schools to have so-called broadband Internet connections, and rather than simply paying one company to do all that, they let out regional contracts to provide broadband to those difficult-to-reach regional areas. And that's worked okay, but you're left with a 256K service and it's not really broadband.

It's really important, Rod Oram says, that we consider what we can do for the players 'that actually does transcend something a bit more sophisticated than a lower tax rate. I'd be reluctant to concede we actually have a high tax rate. Objectively, it's not, and of course it would be nice for it to be lower. I'm all for lower taxes, but for me there's something more sophisticated [that] needs to go on here than just lower tax.' The division between those who see low taxes as the road to salvation and those who do not is deep, he says, and debilitating.

> Take the Irish. Pretty much all the way across their political spectrum they have a very clear, coherent consensus on how to move the Irish economy on, and political debate is only around the edges – a little bit about tax rates or a bit more government spending here or there.

He questions Brash's assessment – 'it's visceral for him' – that the government of Helen Clark is running the country into the ground. If you compare Michael Cullen with Bill Birch he says, you'll find a staggering difference.

> Birch, I thought, was a complete menace. The Finance Minister should not be nickel-and-diming and going into a room for an argument about $10,000. *Jesus Christ*. And he was consumed by that kind of stuff. The Finance Minister is involved in financial

architecture. You are not polishing the woodwork, which is
what he was doing. And Cullen has been very, very good on the
financial architecture.

Of course, architects differ in their opinions. You might say
that, in architectural terms, Professor Tim Hazledine thinks
that we gutted the building in the 1980s and waited for it to
rebuild itself. When you wipe out one manufacturing job in
three, as he says we did from 1986 to 1991, he thinks you should
not realistically expect the survivors to shake off the shock and
flourish – not soon, and perhaps not ever. He takes the view that
we need to be more cautious, less dogmatic, more eclectic in
our policy-making efforts. He also thinks we need to get those
efforts headed in the right direction: *You cannot consume your
way to prosperity; you have to make stuff.* He would like to see us
have a goal of rebuilding our manufacturing sector.

> We unilaterally gave away market access by cutting our tariffs
> ahead of the rest of the world; whereas everyone else in the
> world, they give away market access in exchange for market
> access somewhere else. They bargain. These GATT rounds have
> always been bargaining rounds. People bargaining for access for
> their goods in exchange. We forgot about that and said, *Oh, that's
> bad economics, shooting yourself in the foot . . . free trade is the most
> economically efficient allocation of resources, let's do it.* It didn't
> work. It clearly didn't work.
>
> Only now, more than a decade later, are we recovering from
> that. The shocks of the 1980s. The Muldoon shocks and then
> the Roger Douglas shocks. So I think we need to say, *Well the
> countries that have been spectacular in the last twenty-five years
> and are still being so are the countries that have grown their capacity
> to make things.*

The whole thing about shifting your emphasis towards high-
tech, and the so-called knowledge industries, he laments, is
that 'for an economist it's very hard to get anything out of it that

isn't bullshit. What are they talking about, where's the market failure, and who is not seeing these opportunities now who somehow needs to be shown the light?'

> I don't think it matters what the industries are. If people are making things that have got a future in the marketplace ... then someone's going to make them and someone's got to make them profitably.

Is Hazledine optimistic, then, about the viability of this economy?

> Yeah, I am, but that's probably just because I'm temperamentally sanguine . . . and I look forward to tomorrow. I do think we haven't come to grips with the fundamentals of the idea of sustainability – the idea of being a productive economy being a part of that – making stuff and even the income distribution thing, so I'd like us to worry about those things more.

Rod Oram also has a perception that it takes time for new businesses to emerge from such comprehensive demotion. Before the 'reforms' the economy was very highly structured and that structure was driven by very strong networks. When all that got blown apart, 'we were very slow in rewiring'.

> And it's a very different wiring. So instead of being very industry-oriented, we now talk in terms of clusters or now talk in terms of research consortia between universities, industry and CRIs. We talk about trying to find a way that government can facilitate stuff whether it's the high-growth projects, whether it's the ICT taskforce to grow 100 companies to $100 million of revenue a year. And we're actually only now learning how to do that.
>
> So new organisations like the health IT cluster – because we have got some really interesting companies in health software – [are] only just now [getting their first, full-time paid staff person] to help drive that.

Roger Kerr takes issue with 'somewhat economically illiterate commentary' about 'moving up the value chain to high-tech stuff and all these buzzword kind of things'.

> I say: *God, a log is a really high-tech, value-added product. Start with a seedling and an enormous number of things happen to it before it goes over the wharf.* There's an argument that says there might be some further opportunities for processing it – of course there are in New Zealand. But those are for entrepreneurs to figure out themselves, they are not for governments to have visions about as to what we should be doing. Australia is more, still much more, into commodities than we are. Is there anything wrong with being an iron ore producer? Not with China sucking this sort of stuff up in enormous quantities at the moment. Terms of trade have never been better. It's another myth that New Zealand's terms of trade have been in long-run decline.

You'll naturally get out of industries where you are not competitive 'with the Chinas and Indias and so forth' but, he says, don't be too sure where the markets could take you. 'It could be that the next fifty years [are] the years of the commodity producers. I mean, they are supplying those [booming developing] countries'. So in fifty years or so, where does he see the country?

> I think you've got to try and make a political judgement about that. I would say in economic terms there's absolutely no reason why we couldn't be right back up at the top, like the very top ... New Zealand was there at the time when the tyranny of distance counted far more against us than it does today.

But all of this depends on having a skilled workforce and, well, look at those migration numbers. According to the OECD, almost a quarter of New Zealand's most highly skilled people have left the country – a bigger proportion than for any other developed nation. There's some consolation: immigrants to

New Zealand are more highly educated than the average New Zealander. Best we get them out of the taxis, eh? However, the New Zealanders who leave here are even more highly educated than the immigrants.

So there's a bit of challenge there. But should we be alarmed? You can't expect your very best to stay, can you? This is not the centre of the world. If you aim to be the best in your field, you go to where the field's best are working. Our most viable solution to the problem is probably to try and develop clusters, as various economists have suggested, where we become, if not the best in the world, at least significant in a given field for the people who want to be here.

Beyond that, it really comes down to how well we can manage to do what Rod Oram prescribed – *adapt and thrive*, rather than merely *manage to survive*. If you think you can predict the outcome, a variety of markets will be happy to let you put your money where your mouth is. You might like to start with the market for the New Zealand dollar.

Chapter Seven

DEEP IN THE HEART OF TAXES

10 August 2024

Canberra

Incoming Prime Minister Lachlan Murdoch has pledged to deliver on his campaign promise of a 5% flat tax, declaring that the United States of Australia had big days ahead and an entirely untapped potential. 'People simply were not willing to undertake investment under the yoke of a 14% tax burden,' he said to a jubilant throng of supporters on election night. 'The big end of town finally has something to celebrate. They've been telling us for years that it would throw the election to do this, but they were wrong. The winning streak remains unbroken, even with the Kiwis on board.' Spirits at Labour Party HQ were notably subdued, although one supporter who appeared somewhat tired and emotional had harsh words for his party's campaign: 'Mate, they're mongrels. Not one win so far this century! Not one! How bad is that mate?'

IF YOU fire up your Internet browser and click to www.globalrichlist.com you'll find an intriguing little site. Its purpose may not be immediately clear, but you will see right away that it will probably appeal to people's curiosity. It asks a simple question: *How rich are you?* Then it goes on to say: *Every year we gaze enviously at the lists of the richest people in the world. Wondering what it would be like to have that sort of cash? But where would you sit on one of those lists? Here's your chance to find out.* And this is where the site becomes ingenious: *Just enter your annual income into the box below,* it says, *and click the button that says Show me the money.*

Well. It's hard to imagine that people aren't a little curious by now. So what comes next? For most people, probably, a surprise. Let's suppose you enter an annual income of US$10,000 – not what one imagines most Americans would call a great deal of money. They would get this: *You are in the top 13.26% richest people in the world*, it says, *there are 5,204,294,954 people poorer than you.* And now we find the purpose of the site: *How do you feel about that? –* it goes on to say – *A bit richer we hope. Please consider donating just a small amount to help some of the poorest people in the world.* Should you enter an income of say $100,000 or $200,000, the figures become a good deal more dramatic, and so does the pitch. At an income of $200,000, the site tells you, you are in the top 0.001% richest people in the world and, it asks, *Would you consider donating just a small amount of your enormous wealth to help some of the poorest people in the world?*

Do by all means feel free to make a donation on the site. It might limber you up for what's coming up in this chapter, because if all the invisible hand/Adam Smith/economic rationalist ideology we've just been exploring warms your heart, the territory we're about to traverse may leave you feeling at least a touch dyspeptic. Absolutely shot through with bleeding-heart, lefty, socialist heresies.

Wayne Hope has a certificate on his wall attesting to his foundation membership of the New Labour Party in 1989.

Those were the days, eh? I fetched up in his office because various people I'd been talking to had been expressing their concern that if New Zealand had one particular issue to worry about in the decades ahead, it was the widening gap between rich and poor. He doesn't disagree.

Look at the research of economist Brian Easton, he says. Look at the research by Des O'Dea who wrote a paper on the changes in New Zealand's income distribution for Treasury. The data tells the story: between 1984 and 1996 the gap widened substantially. If you divide the country into deciles you find that the bottom eight all went down in living standards – 'and the lower your decile was, the faster you went down' – and the only people who increased their living standards were the top two deciles. It's not, he says, just one half getting better off as opposed to the other half, 'but a tiny elite getting better off at the expense of the bottom eight. The further you are down the bottom, the worse it is.'

> We can add to that by saying that we have some anecdotal evidence to show that even people on high salaries are not nearly as well off as people who have inherited wealth combined with other investments, capital investments and so on, so they don't have to rely on a salary to live, and those are the people who are involved in the senior levels of corporations of the finance sector, property development and so on – so they are the super-elite.
>
> Down the very bottom – and this comes out in the latest census incidentally – is a . . . segment of New Zealanders who don't even have electricity or a phone and might be living in motor camps or garages, or accommodation which is essentially third world by any other name. The evidence for that you can find if you go to the digital divide section in the census, and they're finding more and more people are without phones and without electricity.

How can those people become part of the 'knowledge society'? he asks. People who can't make ends meet in the official economy, he says are resorting to the underground one – buying and selling drugs, protection rackets, gangs. 'That kind of informal way of making a buck is actually really deeply entrenched in New Zealand, in Auckland, in Otara, parts of Wellington. It's just a way of life with corrosive impacts on the rest of society.'

> Then you don't need me to tell you the health issues facing New Zealand which is the re-emergence of diseases and maladies which were wiped out at the beginning of last century or at least in the forties, and you're getting the odd case of TB, and meningococcal disease. And all of that stuff represents a kind of health issue that could easily be dealt with if you had a public health system supported by a progressive tax system. But in the absence of that, those who fall through the cracks are caught in a vicious cycle of poverty – poor housing, poor health, poor life prospects and so on.

There's more to this, he continues: there's a sharp social separation between New Zealanders – 'like there's two New Zealands. Just in terms of where people live. White flight to the flash schools away from the lower decile schools, and that's class flight as well as white flight'. He sees it in rural New Zealand as well. 'For those who are well off, that outside world is something to be fearful of, and to keep away from, and tell your kids not to go there and all of that kind of stuff, and what that does is it actually undermines the social fabric of society.'

> You lose your cohesion and the whole thing – New Zealand as a country – becomes very uneasy. And this of course is covered up by relentless advertising, nationalistic hype surrounding our sports teams, but underneath there are some real, real problems.

Hope sees a goading and a tormenting in the relentless advertising and consumerism – 'the goods that are advertised and the experiences that are advertised like overseas travel are outside the reach of even ordinary New Zealanders, let alone poor New Zealanders. And among some segments of the population it's: *How do I get that?* or it might be a vicious sense of envy of those who have it: *What you've got, I want.*

Haven't noticed too much of all this in your street? Well, it might be because you and I are living in a different world. The other side Hope sees to this coin is that the consumer society and its relentless advertising has led to a greed and selfishness and narcissism among wealthy people. 'Extreme makeovers, obsession with fashion, obsession with celebrities.'

> We live in a Charlotte Dawson-world and what that leads to is a kind of ignorance about the outside world among those who are well off, because they don't want to know, and so you get these upper-middle-class ghettos. I went to Whangaparaoa yesterday – Waiheke's going the same way. Secluded little ghettos.
>
> And by your magazines shall you know them – you get these glossy, shallow publications that reinforce the consumer and the narcissism that attends on that. And this is where a lot of the horror stories come from – abandoned babies, child abuse. I'm not saying the gap between rich and poor is the sole cause of all that, but it is a major contributing factor to a whole range of other problems.

Our future makes quite a disturbing picture, then. 'It's not meltdown but kind of a deep-seated social malaise if you like, where one part doesn't know how the other part lives. I've noticed it because I'm in my late forties and I was born in the fifties. I have noticed that change and I've written about it.'

> The saddest areas are the ones where working-class culture has disintegrated and you get sickness and poverty . . . in the early sixties when Otara was set up there was full employment in the

freezing works and light industry, and most of those Maori families were two-income families on award rates and overtime. So although there were cultural problems of reconstructing a new Maori society in the cities, economically they were better off than they are now. Porirua was a good example of a multi-cultural working-class suburb and now it's disintegrated into gangs, drugs and crime.

I think New Zealand has gone down a pretty bleak path. I don't think there will be social meltdown – I think there are good things about the country. I think our cultural and race relations are not great but they're significantly better than they are in Australia. And ironically enough, I think the formation of the Maori party is actually a stabilising influence. So I'm not doom and gloom on that. I think there are real problems, but I don't see a Fiji or Sri Lanka situation. Partly because there is such a lot of cultural interaction between Maori and Pakeha anyway, especially in some parts of the country. And also, people like the Ngai Tahu, who are now a major corporation – they don't want any trouble either, neither do Tainui, they're doing fine, thanks very much. So they're conservative forces as well. So you've got radical Maori over here and you've got conservative Maori over there, and you know – you're not going to get a blow-up. It's the socio-economic polarisation that's the real issue.

Green Party co-leader Jeanette Fitzsimons has similar concerns. She thinks the gap between haves and have-nots has increased 'very, very fast in New Zealand in the last twenty years – we used to be one of the most egalitarian societies up until the about the mid-eighties, and the Rogernomic policies have driven that rich/poor gap, in some cases by making the poor absolutely less well off, but mostly by just making the rich enormously rich and holding down the wages and standard of living of the majority at the bottom'.

And of course the level of satisfaction you feel with your personal consumption tends to be a relative thing. If you haven't got a home or you actually aren't getting enough protein, that is an absolute level question; but if it's just somebody [that] can't afford to get a new car every two years and [has] to wait five, then it is absolutely a relative question of whether you feel well off or not. And we've driven more and more people into feeling that they are poor because we've widened that gap between the haves and have-nots.

A stratified society is negative, she thinks, for everybody. 'It leads to higher crime, it leads to destruction of community feeling.'

Once you get a feeling that *Society doesn't owe me anything, I don't have any responsibility, I've been treated like dirt*, you get a lot of very dangerous levels. The countries with the biggest gaps are the ones that have to invest the most in security systems and high fences and electronic alarms and all of that, and I wouldn't have thought that any of us would want it that way. Now you've got gated compounds springing up here as well.

Tim Hazledine notes the resentment that has built as corporate pay levels have ballooned – the CEO salaries, the golden handshakes. 'People say, *How can it be fair that the pay of CEOs has gone up five to ten, fifteen or twenty per cent a year with no relation to performance or anything else. What's fair about that?* Once, he says, major corporations didn't think they should grab the money even if they could – or not so much of it. He senses 'a bit of a revolt against that', notably in Australia, where 'institutional investors have been saying, *No, come on, this is ridiculous*'.

That's a positive sign. People are saying, *Oh, you don't actually need to pay thirty times the average industrial wage to perform as a CEO, fifteen times is quite enough*. And of course I'm glad the people are revolting. Because I think it's in our long-run interest.

He'd love, he says, to see the whole private school system atrophy, 'as middle-class parents say, *Oh, I'm not going to pay*

$12,000-a-year fees, the state school's excellent – I'd just love to see that. That to me would be a sign of nation-building, doing something that keeps us together as a people, that gives us all similar experiences, which I think is very useful – and sustainable'.

Told you we were moving into the lefty stuff. But before you dismiss it out of hand, consider our Prime Minister's favourite political example: Sweden, where the benefits of growth are a good deal more widely distributed than, say, Milton Friedman would recommend.

Critics of the purist more-market economic approach like to present it as an example of a country that tries a different approach to the economic Darwinism that says that the more freedom you give the rich, the better off the poor will be; growth is the thing that will lift everyone's boat, and you'll get the most growth if you keep out of the way – *low tax, no tape*. Put your meddling hand in with high taxes and big public spending, and you'll hold everyone back.

Well, the *Guardian* asked in early 2005, how true is that? What do the numbers say if you compare the United Kingdom – 'a pioneer of neoliberalism' – and Sweden, 'one of the last outposts of distributionism'. They used 'a set of statistics the *Economist* is unlikely to dispute: those contained within its own publication, the 2005 World in Figures'.

So what did the numbers say?

- In 2002 Sweden's GDP per capita was $27,310, and the UK's was $26,240. In only seven years between 1960 and 2001 did Sweden's per capita GDP fall behind the UK's.

- Its current account surplus was $10 billion while the UK had a deficit of $26 billion. Inflation rate? Lower. Global competitiveness? Higher. 'Business creativity and research'? Higher rank.

- It won on 'quality of life' – third in the world, against eleventh for the UK, plus the third-highest life expectancy; the UK was twenty-ninth.

- According to a 1994 UN Human Development Report, 7.5% of Swedish adults are functionally illiterate. The number in the UK is 21.8%.

- In Sweden, according to the UN, the richest 10% earn 6.2 times as much money as the poorest 10%. In the UK the ratio is 13.8.

And yet, and yet. Critics will point to the tax rates in Sweden coming down in recent years. They'll point to some vigorous deregulation in the last decade. It doesn't pay to get too emphatic about these things.

What does Roger Kerr think of income redistribution? 'I obviously want people to be more productive than they would otherwise be, but I think the general welfare story tells you that you've got to be bloody careful.'

> I want to look at welfare as a safety net. I want people to first of all look to their own resources, their savings and insurance and so forth, to family resources, to private civil society resources [private resources], but ultimately a government safety net of some description. Using that array of things where each has got the comparative advantage to deal with personal problems. But it's pretty clear, to be crude about it, [that] the more you subsidise something like dependency, the more you will get it.

If you're wanting to look at the contribution that fiscal policy can make – and Kerr thinks it's really important – then the level and composition of government spending 'has to be a really big issue'. And the nature of your tax regime is a 'really big one as well'. You can finance your government's spending through a bad tax regime, or a good tax regime, and ours he judges 'quite good. The changes dating back fifteen years or so put us again into good standing by international standards'. Upping the top tax rate was a mistake he argues, 'but it's not one of these end-of-the-earth type scenarios'. If you want to gear tax policy to growth then his prescription is plain: 'lower and flatter'.

It's worth bearing in mind, though, that New Zealanders are not unduly burdened by taxes. According to a 2005 report from the OECD, New Zealand's tax burden is amongst the lowest in the developed world. The overall tax rate for a single-income couple with two children earning the average wage is just 20.7 per cent – the tenth lowest out of thirty OECD nations.

It's also interesting to consider that the biggest economic burdens and worries for New Zealanders change over time. Twenty years ago, it was inflation. Fifteen years ago, unemployment. Presently? Probably the affordability of houses for those who don't have them, and worries about long-term financial security: you start with a student loan, you can't get a house, and you don't have enough to retire on.

Little surprise then that both the government and commentators have begun talking about an ownership society. What's not to like? Financial independence improves your life. What might be most interesting to see is whether the debate can encourage people to look beyond a house as the only way of gaining financial security. *Houses good, shares dodgy?* Try telling that to the canny personal investors in Hong Kong.

It will also be interesting to see whether a Clark administration might look a little more Swedish in a third term. For all that critics may have bristled at the redistributing nature of the 2004 budget, this administration seems to have kept the emphasis on the business of achieving and increasing growth, rather than redistribution.

Equally interesting would be the question of how far a government could manage to diverge, if it wanted, from the prevailing economic orthodoxy. Bill Clinton famously chafed at the realisation that any economic policy he formulated would ultimately be rated and graded in the world's dealing rooms. In a global economic village, your room to manoeuvre is only *so* great.

A gloomy interpretation would be that we have surprisingly little autonomy. Wayne Hope maintains we no longer have a national economy: 'The banks and insurance companies are run from Australia.' A lot of our property, he laments, is actually being run from South-East Asia – by Hong Kong, Singaporean and Chinese development companies. All the major corporates that developed in the sixties, seventies and eighties have been swallowed up: 'Carter Holt has been taken over by International Paper, most of Telecom is owned offshore, [the same goes for] electricity, even railways.'

> You look at basic infrastructures, you look at banking and finance – none of that stuff is nationally co-ordinated any more, and what that means is that governments no longer have the clout to deal with social inequality. They don't have the resources to raise taxes, because if they went for corporate taxes the corporately-owned media would gun them down.

Is there 'no alternative', then? Are we hooked into a larger market and beholden to other bigger players? Well, yes, to an extent, but we're not in lockstep. We *could* take some audacious steps if we chose; whether we *would* or not is another matter altogether. Whatever might happen, here's a comforting thought: we'll probably stay somewhere near the top of that rich list.

Chapter Eight

CAN YOU FIX IT WITH A CAN OF WD40?

6 June 2040

Auckland

Retailing giant TradeMeTradeYouTradeAnything announced today it would be building a new mega-warehouse at its Warkworth distribution centre. The company has been under fire in recent weeks from residents of Auckland's northern suburbs for regularly running out of gas masks. The company's Oceania general manager Matthew Farr-Jones said the facility would have capacity to store three months' supplies of all essential life-support equipment: 'We're talking masks, filters, oversuits, climate sensors and bio-security anklets, and all in the full range of designer styles. Aucklanders expect to be able to drive to an outlet within five minutes of their bio-secure pod to replenish vital supplies. We're passionate at TradeMeTradeYouTradeAnything about exceeding customers' expectations, and this facility will make it possible for us to do so.' He added that anyone who had suffered the loss of an immediate family relative as a result of having run short of gas masks would be entitled to five free masks and a stainless-steel patio barbecue and fridge unit on production of a death certificate.

IF YOU want to hear some soothing words of reassurance about the state of the planet, you could do worse than turn to environmental sceptic Bjorn Lomborg. He opened his 2003 Ron Trotter lecture by borrowing a phrase from a Princeton professor: 'we've been running out of oil ever since I was a kid'. There then followed a litany: In the 1920s, the American Bureau of mines warned that there was just one decade of oil remaining. Ten years later, there was another decade left. In 1940, there were eight. Presently, he said, there is enough left for forty or fifty years at the current rate of consumption. Undiscovered resources might – who knows – give you another 100–150 years. And if you want to use shale oil (and trust me when I tell you that Greenpeace most assuredly don't), you've got enough to cover current consumption levels for about 5000 years.

And he goes on to quote the founder of OPEC who said that the oil age would come to an end, but not for lack of oil; just as the stone age came to an end, but not for a lack of stones. So we can all breathe out then? Not so fast, Sparky. Representing a very substantial body of opinion in direct counterpoint to that is the reassuringly sensible-sounding co-leader of the Green Party, Jeanette Fitzsimons.

She offers a less sunny prognosis. In her state-of-the-planet speech on Waiheke at the start of 2005, she echoed the worried predictions people have been making increasingly frequently in recent months: *Peak Oil is coming*. As nightmares go, it's one of your bigger ones. An oil-based economy, the argument runs, doesn't have to deplete its entire reserves of oil before it begins to collapse. A shortfall between demand and supply as little as 10 to 15 per cent is enough to shatter an oil-dependent economy and reduce its citizenry to poverty.

The Peak Oil thesis is that soon we're going to reach the top of the bell curve. After that, there'll be less available oil each day than there was the day before. And it will get ugly. Shortages. Inflation. War. The modern economy runs on oil – not just to run engines but also to manufacture a vast range of goods. And the really happy bit of the news is that we may be very near the peak already. Days, weeks, months – we can't be sure – the argument runs.

Naysayers maintain there will always be more, and that although the bell curve analysis is right, the peak – the day of reckoning – is more than ten years away. It becomes a little problematic when we can't say for certain where it might come, doesn't it? 'Well we're never going to know where it is until we've past it,' Fitzsimons says. 'I think most people agree on that.' If in fact we have thirty-three years as the government is suggesting – 2037, they've said, is their best guess – we still would have a lot of change to make 'and we should be starting right now'. It would be a very good scenario 'if it were true'. Why is it not? Well, 'look at who's saying the opposite'.

You could choose to believe the oil companies, 'but they've got a very strong interest in maintaining the status quo and having people continue to consume'. You could choose to believe the international energy agencies, 'but they get all the data from the oil companies anyway'. You could choose to believe the US government and their geological survey, 'but they've been wrong before, and anyway, if they were to admit that we're very close to Peak Oil then more people might start believing that that's what they're really doing in Iraq'.

So who else is talking who might be more reliable?

You've got the deputy chair of the Iranian national oil company who spoke in Australia last year or the year before and said world oil production is 81 million barrels a day. The combined oil wells of the planet don't have the capacity to increase production by more than one or two per cent above that. Well, it's now, I think, at 82.6 million barrels. We are very, very close to the peak of production and we can't go higher. You've got independent petroleum geologists and people like Colin Campbell and Dennis Mays of the Association for the Study of Peak Oil . . . experts who are independent; they say we are now very close to the peak or possibly past it.

Fitzsimons said 'within ten years' in her speech to give people the most optimistic scenario 'and I've been criticised by some for saying that'. *Within ten years*, she says, doesn't mean it may not in fact have happened in the very first day of those ensuing ten years. 'But I deliberately didn't set out to be scary in the Waiheke Island speech because I think people have got to come into it believing that we've got options or nobody will do anything.'

If you have a leading firm of investment bankers in the United States saying that we may have already passed the peak, she says, shouldn't that give you some pause? When you consider the range of people who have no axe to grind, who are saying it's very close, they strike her as more credible than the people with vested interests like the oil companies 'who have been caught-out lying about their reserves'.

We know that a lot of oil that was actually found in the sixties wasn't reported until the 1970s or the 1980s, in order to get certain tax advantages, so that when you look at the *reported* oil discoveries . . . if you look at when they were actually discovered you find that oil discoveries peaked in the 1960s and declined quite sharply, and they are currently finding about one barrel of oil for every four that you burn. Then if you look at the fact that Shell was actually convicted for fraudulent reporting of its reserves in order to try and keep its share price up – [and] very heavily fined for false reporting – and had to apologise to its shareholders and its share price dropped quite remarkably after that happened. You know: who do you regard as credible?

The point that actually matters to Fitzsimons is not exactly Peak Oil, 'although that's very important', it's the point where growing demand outstrips the capacity to supply. And that might not be identical with the peak, although it may be influenced by it.

> People say: *Look, as the price goes up, people will explore harder and find more and it will be economic to exploit it.* But they forget that it's actually not supply that is the main problem here. Demand is driving at 10 per cent per year at the moment worldwide and China and India are in the process of starting a major acceleration in their oil use.

The oil just won't be available to whoever can pay for it, and when competition builds for that you are going to see some real fun, she predicts. But what if we take that *stone age didn't end for a lack of stones* perspective? Could we put our hope in alternative energies? Fitzsimons acknowledges our relative luxury of options – New Zealand has more renewable energy per capita than anywhere in the world, with the possible exception of Iceland: 'We're not doing nearly enough to develop that.' But, she says, the hard fact is, there is nothing that can replace oil at the rate that we're currently using it.

> The most important thing is to increase our energy efficiency by several times, not 10 per cent or twenty per cent but by several times. The current motor vehicle fleet in New Zealand uses roughly twice as much fuel as it would need to if everybody had [greater fuel-efficiency vehicles] – the hybrid electrics do about fifty miles to the gallon but even a little Fiat Punto does about fifty-three miles to the gallon. What does your average family saloon do? Thirty. What does your four-wheel drive do? So we need an urgent programme to make sure that all cars brought into the country from now on are enormously fuel efficient.
>   We've got to redevelop the rail system, which is more

efficient for freight than trucks; coastal shipping – new shipping technology with wind assistance; better public transport – there are quite a lot of options – biomass is all very fine for transport options, but they're all scaled. People get really excited about biodiesel made from fish-and-chip oil – cooking oil – now that's great, it's a waste product you can use as fuel, but you've only got to think: how many litres of petrol do you buy in a year and how many litres of cooking oil do you buy in a year, to realise that [it's not going to take you very far].

All well and good, of course, but if the rest of the world stands to slip into some uncomfortable degree of chaos over this, what can we hope for to bail out the big users of energy? Is it possible for China's economy to make the change from oil dependency as readily as this country might? Fitzsimons notes it's much more difficult for a less-developed country to raise the capital; but in other ways, to the extent that China is putting in a lot of new plants, it's easier.

The thing that will produce the best outcome for the whole world will be if China and India leapfrog the old fossil fuel-intensive technologies and go straight to more efficient technologies and cleaner technologies, but they're going to need some capital help to do that. And that's actually what the cleaner development mechanism under the Kyoto Protocol is designed to achieve, in that developed countries that are signed up to Kyoto can get carbon credits for helping less developed countries who are not signed up go to cleaner technology than they otherwise would.

Roger Kerr argues that on the whole there is a very large convergence between economic goals and the environmental goals that we all want: *richer is cleaner*. The higher-income countries, he suggests, look after their environments best. 'Firstly, they don't have to trash them to get wood to burn fires to cook their dinner at night. Secondly, they have got better technology, more energy-efficient and everything else, and less polluting. And thirdly, they can afford trade-offs much better to put more emphasis on environmental quality.'

There's a natural kind of curve research, Kerr says, that suggests that once countries get past the level of about $5000 US per capita income, the environmental indicators tend to improve.

How does Fitzsimons see the position of developed countries in this equation? If you're a clean, non-polluting economy, but your claim on the world's resources is still larger per capita, do you remain a problem? 'I think the only fair way to assess it is per capita consumption.' China will end up using enormously more than America, 'and so it should, it's got enormously more people'.

At the moment, people tend to simply look at the fact that China's total impact is growing; China needs some development. They've still got a lot of poverty, they need to develop; it's America that needs to shrink. I think there's two ways of looking at responsibility. One is, well, *Who's caused the problem we've got now?* Because we've already got a problem. China hasn't contributed much to where we are at the moment. And therefore that is the basis on which the Kyoto Protocol says that developing countries will join in, to some extent, once the developed countries, the OECD countries, have taken recognisable action. So far they haven't.

And then the next step is, well, *Who has got the financial capacity to change?* And that again is going to be the richer countries. But the countries where [there is] the greatest technological possibility to change will be in the rapidly developing countries putting in new plants. For example, some years ago China had a massive increase in refrigeration and they chose to use old technology that was quite energy-inefficient and they had to build a massive number of coal-fired power plants just to run those fridges whereas they could have built less power plants if they'd gone for the most efficient refrigeration technology. We have to make sure that kind of thing doesn't happen.

But back to that Peak Oil nightmare. There must be energy alternatives surely? Well, keep an eye on the papers. But don't say you weren't warned. If only Peak Oil were the only thing to worry about. If you've been in a coma for the past twenty years, a quick refresher: the planet is, depending on who you talk to, threatened in a dire way, or not significantly affected, by the problem of climate change.

It seems to be agreed that the Earth's surface temperature has risen by about one degree Fahrenheit in the past century, with accelerated warming during the past two decades. There is less agreement – but any amount of evidence – that most of the warming over the last fifty years is attributable to human activities.

The possible result? A rise in sea level, bringing change to rainfall and other local climate conditions. Change your regional climate and you could alter forests, crop yields and water supplies. Which knocks on to affect human health, animals, and many types of ecosystems. Or not, if you listen to the sceptics.

Try this as an illustration: the Himalayan glaciers which feed the Ganges, the Brahmaputra, the Mekong, the Yangtze and the other great Asian rivers are likely to disappear within forty years. If these rivers dry up during the irrigation season, then the rice production which currently feeds over one-third of humanity collapses, and the world goes into net food deficit.

Jeanette Fitzsimons sides with the preponderance of experts. 'I think you've just got to look at where the vast majority of the climatologists are. I mean the evidence is getting stronger all the time. I don't expect *anybody* is not now saying the climate is changing.'

The argument, she suggests, is only about whether it is human-induced. On that, she says, the argument is getting stronger all the time.

> What the models predicted is happening. And each year that goes past shows the correspondence between the model predictions and what's happening. The big shock that we had in the last year [was] the rate at which the Arctic sea ice is melting – that was a huge wake-up call, because it's very much faster than was expected. It showed that at the poles, climate change is happening faster than elsewhere. Although there were predictions for that in models, nobody had thought that through to the amount of sea ice melting. And of course the worry now is that it won't be possible to stop it even by reducing emissions – that the dark colour of the ocean that is revealed where the ice melts is going to absorb more energy than the ice did because the ice reflected it . . . and that is going to give you a positive feedback that increases the warming. There are a lot of events like that, the tundra melts and frozen methane that is buried in the tundra [is released] and that will produce runaway climate change.

She cites the report at the beginning of 2005 from the IPCC (the International Panel on Climate Change): 'If we don't turn it around in ten years, we won't turn it around at all.' She thinks it's getting 'much, much harder to sustain the sceptic view than it was even three or four years ago'.

> And even people like Lomborg doesn't say it's not happening. He just says it's going to cost more money to fix it than it's worth. And that assumes that the whole process is a linear one. If it's not, if it's a process of accelerating change and passing thresholds that accelerate the change a bit more, and positive feedback loops; well – what price do you put on survival?

Yes. Mr Lomborg. What does he have to say about this? Well, he says we must realise that we can only do so much. Instead of putting the money into measures to reduce emissions and trying to fix or at least arrest the problem, we could use the vast sums involved to invest in clear water and sanitation for the world's poor: you'd get a better return. The problem is, if the gloomy predictions are right, we reach some point of no return where the ecosystem goes seriously out of alignment and we might be wishing we'd been a little more ambitious.

Fitzsimons says we need to think very carefully about all these issues: there's a lot at stake. Everything is linked to everything else. If we run out of oil, if climate change has dire outcomes, what happens to us? What happens to our fishing? What happens to our farming? What happens to our markets?

> What about when our markets can't afford our dairy products any longer – because dairy products are actually a luxury. What happens to Fonterra? Ninety per cent of their output is exported. What happens to our deep-sea fishing? That is the most energy-intensive food production in the world. We'll probably retreat back to coastal fishing, but our coastal fisheries are already under intense pressure, in conflict with recreational and customary fishing and conservation. There's all of that stuff too.

How does Fitzsimons rate our chances? In her head, she says, she's a pessimist, 'and in my heart I'm an optimist'.

> I have to live as though we can do something about these threats and I do live that way, and I have done something about it in my own life and I believe we can do something about it as a country. So I don't waste time sitting around feeling doom and gloom. I'm putting my energy into changing things and I strongly believe that we can. I don't *know* how much time we've got, but I feel that we may have a lot less time than most people think but we can still do *something*. I mean, some of the changes

we need to make, you could make in the next year. Isn't that worth doing?

Tim Hazledine believes we have to think sustainability, to think, *What are we doing now that helps, or enables, or could be replicated?* Are the things we're doing now making it harder or easier? He thinks it's misguided to be resisting environmental and resource management issues. 'I think the Greens are a voice of sanity in that Parliament,' he contends.

If you find, for example, as recent data suggests, that the rate of fertiliser use seems to be lifting up into levels that are giving farms the yields they need by damaging the waterways in the process, you back off. If something's not environmentally viable, he says, 'do something else. Tourism, which I think now has passed dairying as our major exporter, is green and run on sustainable lines.'

There's an element of Russian roulette to all this. How lucky do we feel? If we don't want to gamble, then the sensible strategy is the precautionary principle, which takes the view that even if we're wrong about the assessment of climate change risk, the downside is too great, so you take appropriate measures to fix the problem anyway. Lomborg, of course, argues that it could be a colossal cost. But surely that leads us in the direction of new energy sources and new practices that may have significant potential for future growth? Playing chicken is all very well, but sometimes it might be wiser to keep off the road.

Lurking behind this whole issue is something that you may or may not regard as a problem: consumption. How has it come to this: people seem to be working more hours than ever, and feel less happy with their lot? Welcome to life in the age of the consumer. Or, if you will, 'affluenza', as defined on the American website of that name:

Af-flu-en-za *n.*

1. The bloated, sluggish and unfulfilled feeling that results from efforts to keep up with the Joneses.

2. An epidemic of stress, overwork, waste and indebtedness caused by dogged pursuit of the American Dream.

3. An unsustainable addiction to economic growth.

'The traditional American dream of opportunity, progress, and freedom speaks to the hearts of most people,' they write.

> Yet the recent 'more is better' definition of the dream has many hidden costs. Our way of life depends on a continuous influx of the very commodities that are most damaging to the environment. This is particularly troubling since nearly every other nation in the world is emulating American consumption patterns. As global population increases and consumption skyrockets, we are rapidly depleting the planet's natural resources, degrading its renewable support systems of water, soil, and air, and producing more waste than the Earth and its atmosphere can absorb.
>
> Our hectic work-and-spend way of life also has huge social costs. In 1998, over 1.4 million families declared personal bankruptcy, credit card debt reached new heights, and the personal savings rate fell to the lowest level since the Great Depression. Millions of Americans report feeling exhausted, pressured, and hungry for more balanced lives. They are seeking greater purpose and more free time to spend with family and friends.

If that appraisal strikes a chord, you'll find a wealth of good stuff over at www.affluenza.org. But surely those Americans are far worse than us? Maybe not. Would you say, looking around, that advertising and marketing have a hefty influence on our lifestyle here? Could it be that, just as it is in most modern economies, advertising is advocating pretty ferocious consumption? Could it be that an undue influence on material things is concentrating attention on individual satisfaction and depreciating any interest in community, any interest in altruism, or anything else? Jeanette Fitzsimons thinks so.

The huge emphasis on consumption, she says, is actually reducing the sum of human happiness by downgrading all other sources of personal satisfaction 'and setting up expectations and aspirations that in many cases can't be met, and setting up envy of people who've got more'.

> It's also the chief driver of destruction of the planet because it's overconsumption that is the reason that so many systems are now pushing right at the physical limits of the planet – whether it's water availability, energy availability, ability to absorb pollution, waste disposal, soil [erosion], expansion of desert, it's all driven by consumption.

We talk about demand, Fitzsimons observes, when we talk about economics, 'and so many people think, for example, that the energy issue is an issue of energy *supply*; it's actually not, it's energy *demand*'. She thinks it's had 'a huge effect' on people's relationships with each other and with their communities 'because we are defined as economic beings rather than as family members or citizens and members of communities and so forth'.

'I actually don't believe that the rising levels of material affluence have made us any happier,' she asserts. And underpinning that is an advertising and marketing regime that fuels the envy and the desire, isn't there? 'Absolutely,' she agrees.

Fitzsimons points out another damaging consequence of our preoccupation with consuming things: we're not saving enough. 'We have a very, very low level of saving, therefore we are not generating the capital within New Zealand to invest for the future, therefore we're doing two things – both of which I see are negative.'

We are inviting foreign capital to come in and do it for us, which seems to be selling out our sovereignty – more and more of our coastal land is being bought by people from overseas and more and more of our high-country land is being bought by people who don't have the same ethic of allowing public access that New Zealanders have traditionally had in the high country. More and more of our infrastructure is owned by firms who have actually no loyalty to New Zealand. I see that as bad.

And the other thing it's doing is it's driving us to mortgage the future in order to pay for the present. The level of debt and household debt is actually extraordinarily high, and when you look at assets versus debt, you've got a significant proportion of New Zealanders who have negative net worth and those people are never going to be able to prepare for the future. The future is not going to be like the past; to survive the future we've got to invest in a range of ways now, and we're not generating the capital to do that.

She offers an example: the current focus on transport – particularly roading. She hears people saying that Transit New Zealand and local councils should be able to borrow for roading, leaving the bill to future citizens. 'If you were starting off from that point, that might make some sense, but actually we inherited a fully paid-up road system, paid for in the past.'

We've always used the pay-as-you-go system, where you pay charges which accumulate in order to pay for the new roads we need, and which pay for the maintenance of the existing roads. Now this generation has become so greedy that it sees no problem at all in inheriting a fully paid-up roading system, but wanting to build a whole lot more now than it wants to bother saving to pay for, and therefore borrowing against the future to build more roads.

It's the same as the politicians did to health and education, but particularly to education: a whole cohort of cabinet ministers who got free tertiary education at the taxpayers' expense and who were then expected as high earners to pay reasonably high tax rates so that the next generation could get the same benefits – objected to paying those tax rates, took their free education, changed the law and said, *Oh, students should pay for their own education*, and so now we've got very high student debt, seven billion dollars that students owe the government, that's preventing them from having families, owning their homes, starting new businesses, whatever, [and] driving a lot of them overseas. Ironically, it's starving the country of some of the intellectual capital that we need because they go elsewhere to chase higher wages or to escape debt repayments, and it's having the reverse economic effect of what was intended. It's all about this generation taking what the past generation handed on to it, but not being prepared to hand anything on to the future.

America is perhaps the most extreme example of where this frenzy of consumption takes you. Do they have a greater impact upon the planet? Yes, Fitzsimons says, per capita they have a greater impact than anywhere else 'and that is where advertising, marketing and the god of personal consumption has reached its most extreme – on a per capita basis'. But she points out that the elite of some other countries are now trying to exceed even America. She recounts a story she mentioned in her state-of-the-planet speech:

In late 2004, developers in Hong Kong were about to demolish seven, forty-storey apartment towers, containing two and a half thousand apartments with great views built for low-income folk. The redevelopment was intended to produce a smaller number of luxury apartments. This was the tallest and largest building ever planned for deliberate demolition, producing 200,000 tonnes of waste, to be dumped at public expense. The punch line is that these apartments were brand-new, fitted out, furnished, and just waiting for their first occupants. Amazingly, the story has a happy ending . . . pressure from Green groups in Hong Kong . . . led to the demolition being called off.

'I was just blown away,' says Fitzsimons. 'That was a story that to me symbolised so much of what is wrong at the moment.'

The converse, of course, is that a community that is involved in things other than simply working for money to buy things has more time to engage with one another and do things in the neighbourhood, doesn't it?

> Well that's right, and actually that's another effect of consumerism – it has led to longer working hours: the very thing that the technology revolution was supposed to take in the other direction. We have not got more leisure; in fact, the forty-hour week has become a nostalgic memory. How many people can now keep their working hours to forty hours? The highly paid people – the executive class – are working longer and longer hours because life has become very competitive and they have to do that to keep their jobs and to climb up the ladder, and the low-paid are working longer and longer hours because forty hours on the minimum wage isn't enough to keep a family.
>
> I think I read that the average working day including overtime has increased three hours in the last year. There has certainly been a big increase in the hours that we're working, and of course that has its effects on children; it means that parents are spending less time with their kids, [and] kids are spending more time doing what? Watching television, hanging out with unsuitable company, playing pokie machines, wandering around the malls, or whatever.

Meanwhile, out in the communities, the long working hours are taking their toll in another way. Fitzsimons says the volunteer groups that hold communities together, from the neighbourhood environmental street-care group to the Meals on Wheels or the local sports trust – are all feeling the effect.

> New Zealand does have a tradition of a huge amount of volunteering, which is extraordinarily good at building communities. And it's declining. All the NGOs say it's harder to get volunteers

now because more people who are working are working for fifty hours a week instead of forty.

Climate change, Peak Oil, rampant consumerism. It's all a bit of a bad dream, don't you think? What to do? Whistle, hope for the best, and listen to Mr Lomborg? Perhaps he's right. But as wagers go, this one is betting the farm.

HAVE YOUR SAY

A betting market can be a kind of continuous popular referendum. So what would happen if you had a betting market on aspects of New Zealand's future? Why not open one and find out? This book has a companion website which offers you the chance to place your bets on where we're going.

Go to www.optimisticpredictions.com and you will get an imaginary $100 to wager on each of the fifteen predictions about New Zealand's future. As soon as you place your bet, the market is updated, and the new odds are displayed.

The market offers six predictions based upon this section of the book:

- New Zealand becomes a state of Australia.

- New Zealand's standard of living overtaken by Fiji.

- Oil shortage precipitates worldwide depression.

- Brain drain reaches point of no return: all skilled New Zealanders emigrate.

- Planet loses capacity to sustain human life by 2065.

To place your bet, go to www.optimisticpredictions.com

Plague & Pestilence

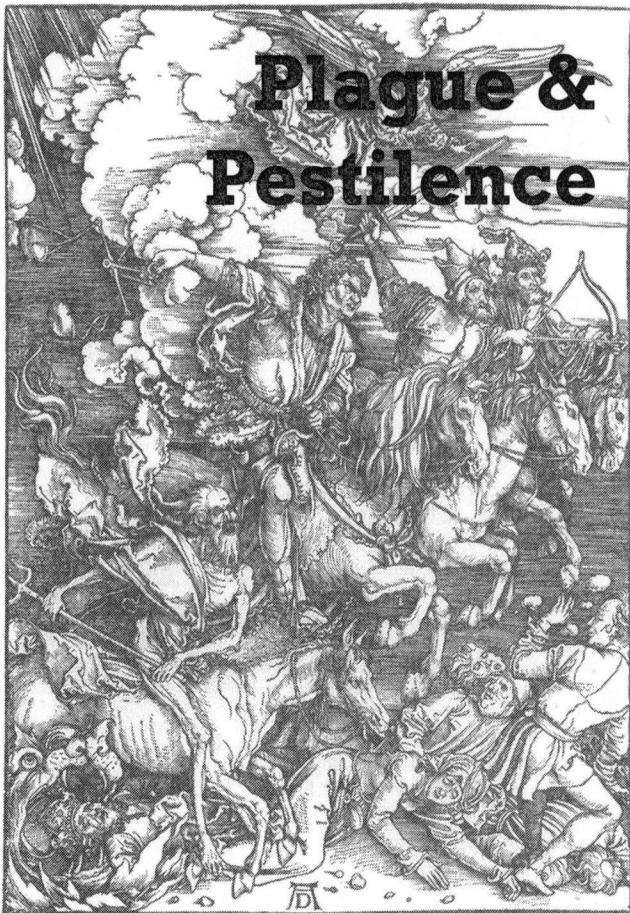

Chapter Nine

4 August 2045

Auckland

The end has come suddenly and embarrassingly soon for the Mt Roskill-born charismatic preacher Tom Bonnet, whose meteoric rise in the past eighteen months is the latest in a scandal-beset series of charismatic televangelist New Zealand preachers. Observers generally track the trend to the rise of the Destiny Church at the turn of the millennium. It enjoyed several years of notoriety, but was supplanted by the end of the decade by the newer and brasher GWB empire of 'Redeemed By Jesus' franchises. Bonnet had emerged as one of the world's most outspoken and celebrated of the GWB franchisees, and there had been talk of his being groomed by the GWB organisation to become one of the first foreign-born and non-US citizens to take advantage of the so-called Arnie Amendment and make a bid for the White House. However, a feather duster, a rubber glove, a milkshake, a senior executive from the McHappy's family restaurant and bar chain, and a hidden camera have put paid, it seems, to all those ambitions.

THERE IS an argument people make that if God doesn't have plans to level California some time soon, he owes Sodom and Gomorrah a big apology. If your God is a wrathful God, then what plans might he have for New Zealand as it descends into a mire of depravity and moral turpitude? Big ones, according to Bishop (at the time of writing) Brian Tamaki. We'll be hearing from him shortly. First, though, an outing, which I first shared last year with readers of my blog at www.PublicAddress.net.

Although a *New Zealand Herald* poll of 1000 New Zealanders carried out early in 2005 revealed 67.7 per cent of people were believers in God, only 20.6 per cent said they often attended church. They say that Christians are the new gays, in the sense that it can be somewhat shameful in these most secular of times to be 'outed' for your churchgoing. I have both believed and not believed in God over the forty-three years of my existence. At our country school we had Sunday school on a Monday in the community hall where we sang songs and listened to stories. I may be mistaken, but as far as I can recall, most Mondays it was the same story about the wise man who built his house on the rocks. These were illustrated with figures on a felt-board. Attendance was voluntary, but typically all the kids except the Roman Catholics trooped across the road each Monday afternoon to get their instruction. In my last year at the school, my brother, sister and I rebelled and chose to bike home instead.

Religion and I didn't see much of each other after that for a decade or two. I got to high school and for a time I acquired secular lefty trappings. I wore a black arm-band for a month when Mao died – and no, I don't feel too clever about that now. Not that there were many takers for that world-view at Feilding Agricultural High School in 1976. That was more or less the point. We read Samuel Beckett and Albert Camus, and I decided existentialism and an absurdist perspective on a Godless world were just what I was looking for.

I went off to university and made new secular lefty friends, and did plenty of, well, sinning. We sat in Legal System and listened to a talented but jaded lecturer offer us a few insights into the typical career trajectory of people such as us. He would get our leftist sensibilities all fired up with the injustice of a case and then he'd drop this on us: *Ten years from now, you'll charge people a lot of money to take the other side of this case.*

Not us, we all protested.

Another lecturer offered us this hypothetical dilemma: A house is burning. From it you can save either a baby or a Rembrandt. *As if*, we all declared. Or rather, all but one. One nice guy called Phil, who was in the Territorials, bravely allowed that he'd save the picture.

Ah, but we're older now. I don't think anyone that I recall from that group would have gone over to the Rembrandt side, but I have to say, the old lefties are thinning out. And I'm not so secular these days. Believing in God comes in handy when you're teaching your daughter's Sunday school class. I've been doing it for two years now, and I expect to be doing it for a good long while. I regard it as balance in her life against some of the other messages she's going to encounter. The Barbie people, the Mary-Kate and whatever-the-other-one's-name-is people, the cell-phone people, Disney, and a few million other grown-ups who ought to know better are all looking for every angle they can find to bombard our daughter and every other child on the face of the planet with their pitches, and I don't care much for their messages. The emphasis is simple: *Develop a taste for acquiring things. Think principally about yourself. Preoccupy yourself with your image. Think shallow: shallow is good. Put yourself first and preoccupy yourself with becoming a consumer.*

I like the Christian values that encourage selflessness, and consideration, and charity, and forgiveness. I think they make the world a little better. I accept that you can get good moral guidance in other ways too; I just happen to like this option. I like the community we have at our church. I like the good humour and the genuine interest people have in each other. And I like the thoughtful reflective context it offers. You have your choice of services: I like the solemn quiet ones. Faith comes in many packages; I'm still working out what it means to me.

Whatever it really does mean to me, I'm not sure – after a visit to the pastor and then to a Sunday morning service – that it overlaps a great deal with the messages being offered at the Destiny Church.

Brian Tamaki says he was twenty-one when his life changed. It was a few weeks after he'd been at a prayer meeting and the preacher had told them all: *Jesus Christ can change your life.* Would he go up and receive Christ, the preacher asked? The 'Mark II-driving, rugby-playing, beer-drinking twenty-one-year-old' didn't think it was his thing. But he went up anyway. He remembers the preacher saying: *Just say this prayer, 'I receive Jesus in my life'*. Nothing really startling happened at first, but five or six weeks later, the twenty-one-year-old, who was working in forestry 'among hard men', had an experience:

> This guy had said, *If you have any doubts about your salvation ask God to reveal himself to you, he will*. I heard that. And I did – in my room. And again, after a short time I asked God: *This is a real good time to make yourself known to me because I am not going to go to church . . . and I appreciate what happened back there and I hope I'm not going to hell.*

He got a response. 'I was dumped on my back and the only time that had happened was when I was tackled in rugby.'

It was just like I was going out of my body, through the roof. I could see the little parachutes that the kids had thrown up onto the power lines hanging on the outside, but I knew I was in my bedroom, but my feet were going through first, and I could see this. I saw a couple of birds fly past and I could see the trees in the wind and I thought, *What the heck is going on down in my body?* and I knew it was God.

It was 'a flip-around'. He stopped smoking, he didn't want to drink any more alcohol, he didn't swear any more ('and I swore like a trooper'). He says he 'just cleaned up internally'. He started to look at people 'with different eyes'. And he started reading the Bible.

I consumed it; I took it to work, snuck it to work, and I worked with a gang of fifteen guys – bulldozers and falling trees – and that's the last thing you put out to these guys, who are doing all sorts of stuff, but it was so dramatic I wasn't afraid. But they all noticed. They noticed the change before I told them. *Something different about you. You've gone all religious.* 'Yeah, I have.' And then I started telling them. I'd get some of them saying, *But what really happened to you? You were like this and now you're like this.* So this whole thing dramatically changed and I just consumed the Bible for a solid year, just read it.

It's quite a thing, coming from *Playboys* and *Penthouses* and suddenly going to a Bible. They were the only things I'd read, if I read at all, and I'd left school at fifteen and I didn't care, I didn't do School C. My mates were earning money and I wanted to do the same so I went straight into the workforce. But here I was.

But the thing about it, he tells me, was that he could read it and somehow get 'the story behind the story'.

I could interpret it in the light of now and I think this is why my ministry today, if I can say it, has so much value for people where they are now. It is able to galvanise and catapult the church, I think, into a new day.

Which, it turns out, is most timely, because the churches need to wake up 'or we're going to be overtaken by secular humanism, liberalism and all this sort of stuff. And unless we do something now we are going to sentence our kids to a dangerous future.'

Glad you mentioned that, Brian – can we talk about the notion that the best way to give everyone the chance to practise their religious freedom, to be able to pursue their faith without persecution, is to say there will always be a part of life that is entirely secular so that no matter what faith you are, everybody is bound to follow it? Well, he says, everybody's got an agenda, whether they like to admit it or not, a philosophy of life, an ideology that they adhere to:

> For me, secular humanism, for instance, which is mostly what the government and a lot of the present political parties in government are, they are secular humanist, which is a religion. It is a religion. No matter what they say, it is a religion because it affects their belief system, and so whatever ideology you adhere to, that means there's something in you that's got to believe in something that gives you your so-called value system or your principles to live by in life; and whether it's secular humanism or liberalism or atheism or Christianity or whatever, somebody's going to impose their agenda and their philosophy on life on people, on society.

It's a matter of what you believe is the truth, he says. He believes Christianity is the ideology that has the best components to set you up for life. It beats all comers. But it has competition and it needs to win the argument.

> Everybody else has come out of the closet. The Greens, the tree huggers, the pot smokers, the liberalists, you know, the homosexual community, the secular humanists. Those people have come out, they have activists, they strongly believe the ideology,

they are motivated people, they use the media to basically bring that message into society and that's how you capture the masses. And the masses, if they don't have a guiding principle, or an anchor for values, they just believe what they are bombarded with.

But if we take, for example, homosexuals, is he saying that they want people to emulate them? He thinks every ideology wants acceptance. 'That's part of any belief system, it wants acceptance. Acceptance comes through, you know, entrance or exposure into the people market, the public domain.' The media, he says, is a very powerful tool – 'to infiltrate it would be a very good thing'. Media conditions the cultural climate of the day. 'There are some people in there who pull the strings and have certain connections and can influence a lot of people.'

But to get back to this separation of church and state, Brian . . . There is, he concedes, a separation in the sense that the church is not to rule society, 'but it is interrelated because you can't separate morality and the church, and you can't separate the domain of economics, education, really'.

I mean if you do, then we are non-existent, then they are saying the Bible is not an authority, which secular humanists want to do. They want to push the Christian message right out of the public domain, I know. That's the agenda.

He's not here, he says, to be a politician, 'but I am definitely here to oversee the word of God's entrance and its plumb-lining over all aspects of life. I guess you could say I do see that God's desire is to permeate the whole of society with his values, to put it in a nice way.'

And would Brian say that God emphatically proscribes homosexuality? It's but one of many behaviours, he replies. 'There's many others, of course, just as much as adultery or immorality, sex before marriage. We're having 250 kids this

Friday taking an abstinence vow. People have fingered me as being a person who hates gay people and that, and that's not so. That is just an issue.'

What about this civil unions legislation, then? What seems to be the problem? Well, it's the homosexual agenda that's trying to legitimise itself by legislation that he doesn't agree with. He says he's never going to stop adultery and immorality and homosexuality, 'and that's not my call', but to legislate this as a law – that's going too far. Enough is enough. He can see 'the education system then, once it becomes law, then the hate speech law will be following next, it's like the Swedish pattern'. And he doesn't want our nation to end up like Sweden. Over there, the education system teaches that it's against the law to discriminate against homosexuality as an odd sexual behaviour. So they must teach it as being on the same level as a hetero-sexual relationship. 'And I don't want [my] grandchildren sitting in school with a little boy who's told it's alright for him to sleep with another boy. Or a girl to have a lesbian relationship with another girl.'

Does he have any statistics on the effect of that, by any chance? It's 'too early to predict that now, but this is how society lives'. He doesn't wait for stats to come through 'because that's always after the fact'.

> I work on revelation and just God's knowledge, and He knows and I know without a doubt right now that it's a dangerous social activity to be legislating, and I am not willing to stand by and say, *Wow, it's just the times,* and let people have their own choice, because half the people don't know what to choose and so you've gotta be up there contending.

That's an interesting point because the church doesn't just stop at the door on Sunday. It provides crèches and education and training and welfare and a whole-of-life service, all potentially exerting a powerful influence on people. If half the people don't know what to choose, could they be pretty suggestible? 'God did not give us ten suggestions,' he says, 'He gave us ten *commandments*.' Society's big problem is 'secular humanism, which is the dethroning of God and the enthroning of man'. It's *me*-ism he says. People don't want to be told that *This is the way to walk and this is right and this is wrong and this is good and this is bad.* People, he laments, want to be able to say what is right and wrong for themselves.

> In actual fact . . . that's one of the worst philosophies of life that any intelligent human being could even think to try to adopt, because it just destroys and we have seen proof of that.

God, he says, gave us the Ten Commandments, he gave us some principles of life, and Brian is an extension of that. 'I am a messenger so I do preach values and there is definitely absolute right and wrong and there is good and bad.' No, a lot of people don't have those values systems, 'they don't have tracks to run their life on'. He's not afraid to say that a part of his ministry and all his job is to be able to tell people how to live. 'And not only tell them, but be a model of that. Here's my family, here's my marriage, here's my three children, here's my grand-children.' You may perhaps be relieved to hear there are parameters to this. For instance, he doesn't go and say, *This is the toothpaste you use.*

> If people want to leave they are free to leave. If people want to join they are free to join us, it's their choice. I don't tell people who to marry. It's quite amazing actually that in quite the opposite to what the perception is, everything is by choice. You choose to be here. You choose who you are going to serve. You choose what your future's gonna be. But here, this is what I am putting out here, this is what God says about this. But you got to choose it.

You are always, he says, going to get people who for whatever reason choose to reject God, religion, Christianity, the Bible. That's their choice, 'but it doesn't mean to say that they are right. Just because two adults consent to a relationship and it's unmarried, doesn't mean to say it's right. Because two men or two women consent to a relationship, doesn't mean to say it's right.'

Brian Tamaki guesses he can admit that there are certain ideologies 'that have managed to penetrate society in a way where it's probably dislodged or displaced the Christian ethic'. He sees his mission as a kind of reformation.

> It's not a grandiose thing to me, it's just a necessity, and the timing is so right and the season; and everything that's happening in politics and in the country and just right down to the ordinary man in the street that I talk to and my neighbours, they are all saying the same thing: *We are tired of this liberal stuff that we are getting poured on us.* The ordinary man doesn't like what's going on, by the way, he just doesn't have a vehicle to express it.

What are some of the things he thinks worries the ordinary person most about where we are right now? The everyday New Zealand man and woman see that there is 'a definite agenda by this present Labour Government that is anti-family.' He cites the lowering of the drinking age, the decriminalising of prostitution, 'of course the Homosexual Law Reform Bill that's well gone and almost a million petitioners said *Don't do this,* and four or five people around there said *We're gonna do this because it's our agenda*, and they pushed it through.'

> If you go just to the ordinary person, go into somebody's lounge, you put this stuff before them, they don't want it. They do not like what's going on. For instance, when we made that stand for the Civil Union Bill, most people I talked to didn't really

understand what the Civil Union Bill meant . . . because the media put [it in] this flowery language and complicated a very simple issue. The issue was there are two men and two women want to get together and be accepted and eventually want marriage status, that's the truth.

So when we came out I just put it in straight language. *Two men and two women get together, it's unnatural*, and they go, *Ahh, I got it*. And that's what I got around the street – *You actually made us aware that this is an issue that we don't want* – and you know how the man on the street puts it, and he's neither pro-Christian or pro-secular, he says, *I don't want this homo stuff for my kids*. That's it. That's his language. Now that's 80 per cent of the population. I've got contacts and networks all round the nation in every town and every city, and that's the general talk. You're talking about a minority here – 10,000, at the most, people involved in the gay community who have pushed this agenda so far – I take my hat off to their determination. I tell you what, the Christian community; two million of us registered ourselves in the census as religious or Christian. Now two million, over two million. That's the voter pool I am stirring up right now.

People, he laments, are very accepting. He sees them being conditioned by the media and 'this liberal government'. That's the real agenda, he says, 'just put it out there, put it out there, put it out there; until after a while, it's normalised and then it's accepted and then they legitimise it and then legislate it'.

I am really concerned about that very lackadaisical attitude of New Zealanders that, because I think we classify as one of the most liberal nations in the world, people just say, *That's alright, I don't mind if two people beside me are sleeping with sheep or with each other or, you know, whatever they're knocking up. But as long as it doesn't come over my fence*. It's a crazy idea. It honestly is, and if you say to them, *Well, little Johnny here, is that your son, how would you like him to be sodomised?* [They say:] *Oh, I'll kill them if they do that*. So I say, *Well hang on, that's happening*.

It will only be a matter of time before the door opens.

I don't think that the normal or average New Zealander has a vehicle, a voice. He just gets a *Herald* thrown at him and a TV programme, documentaries, you know, *Queer Eye for the Straight Guy* and *Shortland Street* . . . billboards, everything just bombards . . . people get so drenched in it that they relent cos they've got no – well you just think of somebody that has no moral anchor.

Talking about family, would he say that there is a fair definition of a family that's wider than just mum and dad and the kids – an extended family? No.

Family is God's idea. Marriage is God's idea. It's not up to be contested, to be negotiated, to be discussed whether it's valid or not, whether other relationships – there is no other relationship that is equal with marriage. A man is a male and a woman [is] born a female. You cannot be born male *or* female. If you're a female you can't be born a male, and homosexuals and lesbians are not born. That is the only relationship that can procreate and reproduce, and it's the most stable relationship proven over time that is the best emotionally, physically and spiritually and mentally to bring up the next generation of children, their offspring. Proven.

But sometimes there's a better environment for a kid than the one they are in, surely? He accepts that there are going to be some people who are dealing with problems and issues in life, but 'it doesn't make marriage wrong because a husband and wife are arguing or because there's divorce and separation'. But isn't a family what you make it? An aunty on her own or a grandmother? Well, if it's the best suitable thing, yes, he says, but it's not the ideal.

It's proven that every child, [knows that there's a] feminine side and [a male one:] male and female, father and mother – I mean, you know, a child *knows*. If it had its choices, early in its life, it wouldn't want any parent to divorce or separate. And it wants a dad *and* a mum. There's aspects of the creation of those two particular species and genders that we need for a proper balance.

So how does he account for the poor survival rates of marriages? Where did we go wrong? The day we threw God out of the equation, he answers. 'The day this nation turns back to God is the day you see a whole lot of right things happen.' He says the schooling Destiny offers will turn out children 'ten times better than kids in the state schools. Our social services and what we do with the young people, it's proven now these kids have left a life of drugs and alcohol and sex before marriage and they are happy kids'.

Does he see himself being more political than evangelical in the next few years? He thinks the church has been its own worst enemy.

Somehow we got neutral on political issues, we got neutral on morality, we handed that over to the world, we got neutral on family issues, we gave [it all] back to the world and these were all original from God's perspective, this was His domain. Marriage was God's domain. The whole education system started from Christian principles. So did the hospital and health care.

He's adamant that this is not the church going into Parliament in Wellington. 'I don't want to be there. But we will definitely have influence on what shapes the policies and principles and how [the] nation and the people are going to be run.' Someone has to interpret the Bible and 'download its revelation, and you give that to those who've been called to politics and the executive of that in particular'. He envisages officials saying, *Hey, this is good, this is common sense. That's how we are going to build a great nation.*

He's an affable man, and there's a look of anxiety in those evangelical eyes that he's going to be pilloried by yet another journalist. I ask him if he's modelled his work on the whole-of-life philosophy of the Ratana church. No, actually, he would like to think it's the spirit of John Wilkes Booth.

Salvation Army? Maybe, but when I make my way to a service a month later, I'm not sure that that's the spirit I encounter.

You can see before you even reach the church that this is quite an enterprise. There are – count them – six people in white gloves and fluorescent jackets directing traffic to the many car parks outside the church. In you go, to find the auditorium filling quickly. The two thousand-odd seats face a stage with massive video screens behind them. Earnest-looking young men patrol the aisles, serving as ushers but also managing to impart some of the bouncer cred that a stern expression can win you.

While we wait for the show to begin – writing in hindsight, 'service' doesn't really capture it – I chat to Barney, a genial middle-aged fellow who came here from the New Life church back in the early days. Then, the Destiny Church was just a couple of hundred strong. He's been here ever since. A builder, he's been a regular at the many working bees. He likes the feeling of community. And now the music starts. It's quite an opening. Thirty in the choir, a dozen in the band, and these guys can SING. The house is rocking.

Once the singing is done – and that's all of half an hour – it's time for the most in-your-face collection I've ever seen in a church. Up on the ten-foot video screens go pictures of coins and notes, just in case you're not quite sure what you need to fish out of your pockets. Then we get the instructions: there are two collections – one to fund the TV and Internet broadcasts worldwide and one to fund the 'planting programme' for new churches springing up around the country. We're exhorted to brandish the coin we'll be dropping in the bucket, and up go two thousand compliant arms. Any comparison with Nuremberg begins and ends here. Whatever else happens at this church – and as we'll shortly see, there's no shortage of the political in this putative place of worship – the prevailing mood is of *family* rather than *rally*.

I try to gauge the composition. More female than male and more brown faces than white – my guess would be Maori and Pacific Islanders making up perhaps 60 per cent of the congregation. There are older children, a fairly significant number of young adults, and then a fairly even distribution of ages past that. They're dressed smartly. Many carry their Bibles and notebooks. There's a welcome for new members to have coffee afterwards – *And why don't you raise your hands*. Perhaps a dozen go up. There's the general housekeeping, a song or two more and then it's time for the headline act.

Up comes Pastor Brian – the elevation to Bishop is still ahead of him, but as we now know, destined – and he is beaming. Wearing brightly shining rings on his fingers, he laughs often. He invites us to tell the person next to us, *I like the smell of the perfume you're wearing, I like the smell of your breath*. I look at Barney and the young Samoan guy alongside me and wonder if this will be a good remark to offer in a church that feels quite so much antipathy towards men who take a strong interest in other men.

And off we go on a sermon that will prove to run for – I don't know: an hour and a half?

We begin with one of the tenets of secular, rational science – that nature abhors a vacuum – which is pressed into service to explain how vulnerable we are to the predations of the Devil.

In any given spot, you'll find either the Devil or the Lord. Lord goes out, Devil comes in. Not surprisingly, the Devil is in places like SKYCITY, and the housie, and the bars, and the places of prostitution where the whoremongers go. But that's just for starters, we learn. You'll also find him at the Labour Party, the National Party, the ACT Party, the Greenies and the Maori Party. Oddly enough, I missed a reference to New Zealand First. Some mistake, surely?

It's church, Jim, but not as I know it. Back at our Anglican church in Devonport, the sermons don't tend to engage so much with the notion of 'tearing down the principalities' and taking on the 'organs of secular humanism, and liberalism'. It's a big year, Pastor Brian says, he can *feel* it. Gonna be a showdown. And soon we're plunging headlong into material that sounds surprisingly familiar to this political speechwriter, in an alternative universe kind of way. Much of it makes the proposition that the Devil is dwelling in the institutions of government but the Lord's time is at hand and the Destiny Church is going to take on the institutions and win. This year, no less. The Lord's law is above all else, and this year, 2005, is going to see the battle. New Zealand, he declares, is takeable and we're gonna to take it.

He decries the Relationships Bill and another piece of legislation that he says will outlaw political speech in New Zealand churches. He hates the idea that we could go the way of Sweden where churches can't use hate speech. And he's not too wild about what the other churches are doing to stem the evil tide. They're weak for not taking on the problem – they do a few funerals and that's their lot, apparently. Meanwhile, the Devil's cranking up the magazine printing presses. When the laws change, there'll be *people having gay marriages, men marrying men, women marrying women all over the country and pictures of them kissing.*

It begins to become clear why the young'uns aren't here. We get a fairly steady stream of references to 'sexual perversions'. We learn that 45 per cent of San Francisco is gay and full of the spirit of the Devil and we learn that the traditional churches have been derelict in their duty. They have youth groups where the kids are told – and if it hadn't been inappropriate, I'd have considered asking Barney to pinch me at this point – that sex before marriage is out but it's okay for the kids to kiss, to 'stick their tongues down their throats', and – no, really – to 'have penetration just as long as there's no transference of fluids'.

I am now quite certain that I am in a church like no other. He tells us a little story about driving down the road the day before past a Buddhist temple – it made him want to spew he shares with us. He couldn't believe that ordinary New Zealanders would condone this false idol worshipping.

Oh, but he loves the people, just hates what they're doing. We all do, he reassures the congregation – and they'll bag us for it, but you have to have courage to wear your shield. You have to take it when they call you 'poor', 'wrong side of the tracks', 'Nazis'.

The passion! The bile! The *time*! It's already midday. Pastor Brian has come to the end of a long tirade against the institutions of secular humanism. But the abiding impression I get is not of a political movement being mobilised. This is a church where you concur loudly, and often, as the pastor speaks. Much of the concurrence sounds dutiful. The truly spirited concurrences come when he talks about the locales where addictions of various categories tend to flourish. Gambling. Drinking. Whoring. That gets the real response. The abiding impression here is that this is – for many – a support group for people who have been burned by the various addictions that take lives off the rails. It's a church that puts people back on track, and not-withstanding what other fault I might find with their method, I can't fault that.

But the rest of it? The politics? The evil gay tide? It resonated, but it didn't seem to be the thing that really struck a chord. Still, the service is nothing if not directive. If they want to get people somewhere for an event, they will come. If they want to stage a march, their people will be there. But when the marches assemble, what purpose do they truly serve? Demonstration? Rally? Or marketing drive?

These sorts of issues do make people feel particularly righteous. If you can march into heaven while everyone else is marching in the other direction, there's an appeal to the whole thing. In this uncertain world, vulnerable people with certainty in their life will warm to this kind of thing.

We shouldn't overlook the fact that this present political cli-mate, with its market forces and contracted welfare state, has left something of a vacuum to fill for churches doing good work in welfare and helping out people in need, as Destiny does. They have a crèche, they have a welfare support system, they have a family for people who are hurting.

But there could be an inherent limitation to this kind of movement. Fundamentalist religions, Andrew Sharp asserts, are wrong. They are based on narrow views of human and scriptural authorities and they die: 'They have to be seen as adjustment cults and they always have been.' It's no mistake, he says, that these things occur a lot in the States, because there is huge turmoil, change and uncertainty there – and for many followers, nowhere else to turn.

People have worried about the sinister echoes they see in row upon row of black shirts marching down Lambton Quay. I'm not so sure. These are not people deeply moved by the political rhetoric. It's theatre. Russell Brown was unmoved:

> I think that part of the reason that liberals like me *do* look down their noses at Destiny Church, to be honest, is because it seems *tacky*. It does seem very cheesy. You've got this guy with his slicked-back hair and his sunglasses and he's hamming it up – it's almost like bad play-acting. And when you see him up close, it's even more so. And you've got the guys with the little earpieces in their ears and you think, well, *What are the guys with the earpieces defending against? It's all theatre.* And it's theatre that's effective for their market, but to the rest of us it looks cheesy, and maybe that will be a limit on their growth.

He points out that although we got very excited about the *Enough is Enough* march and various commentators have perceived a rising moral backlash, we may have a skewed sense of proportion.

> There were – what? Maybe 5000 people max on the *Enough is Enough* march. We tend to forget that in the 1970s, SPUC could gather 10,000 people for a march, and did so. And so the idea that there's something happening now that is of greater magnitude than happened in the 1970s when people were saying that society was going to fall because of the Homosexual Law Reform Bill or because of abortion being legalised, it's just not true.
>
> When you look at who was on that march, that was about it, that was about as many people as they were going to muster, I think – but yet, it's still, it's *effective*. It's a big presence on the street and it's the kind of presence of people that you're not going to get on the other side of that sort of issue, where it is the *live and let live* thing. No one is *that* exercised on the other side of the issue that they're going to get into the street, apart from a few hundred gay rights protesters, and good luck to them; but your average New Zealander who has shopping to do or something else, but thinks that it's only fair that gay people get to establish their relationships, isn't going to go out and

march for it, and isn't necessarily going to circulate a petition or something like that.

Brown notes that even right-wing think-tank the Maxim Institute euphemises much of what it says. It tries to put things in secular scientific terms and studiously avoids talking about anything spiritual, 'even though when you look at it, that's what they're talking about. People are a little wary about people who bang on about God.'

Chapter Ten

EVERYTHING BUT THE GOAT

4 August 2025

Auckland

Devonport man Paul Service became the first person to take advantage of the Cross-Species Union Act by marrying his goat in a ceremony on Mangawhai Beach today, flanked by his two most cherished surfboards and dressed in his favourite board shorts. 'Ever since they passed the Civil Union Bill I've been saying that if you love something, you should be able to marry it. I was a bit gutted they wouldn't let me marry the longboards as well,' Service said.

LET'S TALK about numbers. If you happen to run a current affairs show on TV around seven o'clock, there's a fairly good chance you'll be quite keen on those phone polls. It gets the viewers involved, it makes a bit of handy cash, and most importantly *it lets people know how we all think.* Oh, the humanity.

Let's line up a bunch of numbers all relating to the Civil Union Bill. First some self-selecting ones:

- 95.5% of select committee submissions opposed the Bill; 4.5% of submissions supported it. In total, there were 6170 submissions.

- A phone poll on the CloseUp at Seven show, Thursday 2 December, reported that 75% opposed the Bill and 25% supported it. There was a total of 17,463 votes.

And now let's compare it with some scientifically conducted ones:

- A One News/Colmar Brunton poll on civil unions found that 34% thought the Bill should not be made into law in any form.

- An ACNielsen poll found 68% were in favour of same-sex relationships registration.

- In June 2004, a 3 News poll showed over 50% support for civil union. In September 2004 a *New Zealand Herald* poll showed support at 56%.

So what do we have here? A nation of two million or more, as Brian Tamaki suggested, fearful of their children being indoctrinated and subjected to depravities? Or a rather greater degree of tolerance for a measure that's simply designed to give people some recognition?

Let's summarise, first, what the fuss is about. A civil union simply gives you a piece of paper from the State that recognises that you have a formal relationship with your partner. It's registered under the law, it gives legal status to a one-to-one relationship, and it's open to different-sex and same-sex partners.

With your piece of paper, you will now be able to get a bundle of different rights recognised in your status as a partner, once a companion bill is passed. That's the Relationships Bill, which at the time of writing had just passed its second reading. It has two main purposes:

- to make sure that existing legislation is consistent with human rights laws by amending existing laws that unjustifiably discriminate on the grounds of marital status or sexual orientation;

- to recognise civil unions by amending existing laws to provide civil union partners with similar benefits, protections and responsibilities to married and de facto couples.

As things currently stand under the law, there are more than 100 ways that same-sex and de facto couples are treated differently, and generally disadvantaged. The Relationships Bill amends various laws to recognise civil unions and ensures civil union partners have the same benefits, protections and responsibilities as married couples. As well, it explicitly defines a 'de facto relationship' and ensures de facto couples generally have the same benefits, protections and responsibilities as married couples and civil union partners.

In essence, you're giving a bunch of rights to people who have been denied them simply on the basis of their sexual orientation, or the way they've chosen to form a relationship with their partner.

The legislation applies to both heterosexual and gay couples, but as far as the critics are concerned, it's just one sector they're worried about, and it ain't the straights. But how much support is there for the critics' point of view? Are New Zealanders really so worried about the gay menace? Russell Brown cites a study by Richard Bowman of Victoria University in 1978: 'He went out and asked New Zealanders what they thought about homosexuality – the first time anyone had done this in New Zealand or Australia.'

And surprise, surprise, New Zealanders were relatively liberal

– 94 per cent of them said that what people did in private was their own business. And yet this was at the time where Parliament had fairly emphatically rejected a move to remove homosexual acts from the Crimes Act – more than once, I think, it had been voted down and there were all sorts of stern speeches about moral decline and the descent into the abyss and all that sort of thing. It didn't turn out to be what the public actually thought.

He surveyed nearly 500 people in the inner suburbs of Wellington, where you would expect people to be liberal, but also in Hamilton, and there actually wasn't that much difference between the results. Three-quarters of his subjects thought homosexual acts should be removed from the Crimes Act. That took eight more years to happen. Eighty per cent of the people surveyed said the Human Rights Act should be extended to offer protection to people on the basis of sexual orientation. That took *fourteen* more years. So it's quite striking, and I think if you look you find many other instances where the government is following rather than leading society in that sort of thing. By the time the Property Relationships Act became law, there were 300,000 people living in de facto relationships. What's a government supposed to do? To pretend it's not happening? Hide under the covers? It actually *had* to do something. I mean, for all the agonising and weeping and wailing, the government actually had to do something to address that.

Does this in some way speak to the pragmatism of New Zealanders? A pragmatic condition that says: *If you don't bother me, I won't bother you?* Brown suspects we saw exactly that in a *New Zealand Herald* feature on the debate over civil unions. 'There was a kind of *live and let live* attitude in that. A number of people they interviewed in depth said: *Well, I don't like the idea of that – it's not my thing, I'm not that keen on it, but people should be able to do what they want to do, if it doesn't affect me.*'

He thinks a lot of our great social experiments – 'and maybe this is what differentiates us from a lot of other countries – our great experiments didn't spring from theory, we're not big on theory – they came from practical considerations'. We used to be considered the social laboratory of the world, from the late nineteenth century, 'and people would come here expecting to find us able to discuss this sort of thing and they would be horrified to find us quite devoid of theory! We've done these things because there seemed to be something that needed sorting out and then we just got on with it.'

He notes a striking generational difference in attitudes to homosexuality. Anyone in their twenties now, unless they're associated with a church, will 'struggle to see exactly what the issue is'. In the civil union debate, the youth wings of the five parties all came out in support. 'That was extraordinary. I don't think it's ever happened before. And it wasn't just that they disagreed, it was just that they couldn't understand how it was an issue . . . I think young people now find the idea that homosexuality in my lifetime as an adult was illegal is remark-able.' And yet the people who bashed Matthew Shepard to death in Wyoming for his homosexuality were only late teens, twenty, themselves. Is America different?

> Yes America *is* different – every survey of public beliefs shows it has a degree of religious adherence that's normally only found in third-world states and failed states. It's quite extraordinary and you go across the border into Canada and it's completely different. In attitudes towards homosexuality as measured in similar surveys – Pew [Research Center] surveys for instance – America stands out from the rest of the world in that respect.
>
> I don't quite know why it is, whether it's still harking back to the puritan founders or what; but then again, if you read someone like Eric Schlosser in *Reefer Madness*, he demonstrates quite amply that what is said in public in America and what is done in private – the two things are absolutely different. Porn

– enormous industry in the US. But he also points out that before pornography became a big moral issue, there was this rather practical thing – there would be these travelling roadshows of blue movies that men and their sons would go to, and it wasn't controversial then, and then it became controversial and the industry got bigger and bigger – as things become controversial, their use takes off.

The church figures large in America's perspective on this, clearly. Why is it that they're so agitated about it? Brown surmises it might be due to the rise of a different kind of church – the evangelical churches. 'Even though America may be a very broadly God-fearing nation, it's the rise of these particular, more-politicised, more conservative churches that has brought this to the fore.'

He suspects in America, particularly, the issue of redemption is very strong. It's okay to have been a drug addict if you've been redeemed, and he thinks the same issue could be at play in the 'homosexual rescue' movement.

A really common tenet in these churches is that homosexuality is a choice. And if you push them they'll say, *Well, perhaps there's a predisposition but people can still choose not to be.* And of course all the research says that choosing not to be is really just a form of denial and creates further problems down the line. That's a really consistent thing of those churches, is that you can be saved from it. Because if you can't be saved from it, then they'll have to grapple with the issue of *God made me a homosexual* – and that might be difficult to cope with.

I thought Nandor Tanczos' speech at the second reading of the Civil Union Bill was really interesting because as a Rastafarian he reads the Bible and he said, *Well, yes there are a few biblical injunctions against homosexuality – roughly as many as there are against usury. And we don't see people marching in the streets against banks charging interest on mortgages.* Whereas you could say that Islamic societies actually live that out a little more honestly, and Islamic banks have various ways around what they see as usury – around charging interest – and we just kind of conveniently ignore that.

If we take that person with the *live and let live* attitude though, and then we take a couple who've been trying for ten years to start a family and are looking for IVF treatment – if they find, after the relationships legislation passes, and that notionally gives gay couples equivalent rights to whatever will be provided to couples seeking IVF treatment – it's a rationed commodity and you know that every person who's involved in that is very, very agitated about it; is it possible that you're going to see some kind of a dust-up that we haven't yet seen, where live and let live is fine, but if people are finding that they are likely to lose out in the queue to a gay couple, are we going to see them being less tolerant of people of a different orientation?

> Yeah, that's quite possible. I think the adoption one is going to be more difficult and it's going to take time. And to be honest, I'd like to see it take time. All the sensible research shows that it doesn't make any difference – the main thing is that kids have someone to protect them and love them. Yet from my point of view, I've got a great deal of respect for the ability of women to nurture children. I have less awareness of the ability of men to do that . . . So I think justifiably that's going to take a little longer, and I think we'll have to proceed slowly and see what happens.

Brown's never met a same-sex male couple raising a child, 'whereas I've known lesbian couples who've done a great job'. It'll be interesting, he says, to see how many gay men do want to go through it, 'because I think the first few who go through it, it'll be fairly fraught. And I think it actually should take some time to bed in . . . just because there *is* no track record of that. Leaving aside sexual orientation, there's not much track record of – certainly compared with what there is with women – of men caring for children from infancy.'

There's a slippery-slope argument critics make that we should probably deal with at this point. This is the *If love doesn't discriminate and neither should the law, well, I love my goat, why can't I marry it?* argument. Actually, if we go back fifty years in some parts of the world, you'll find people made this argument over interracial marriage. Times change, people learn. Anyway: to the argument. To make it, you have to ignore the distinctively human capacities that sexual relationships entail. You have to reduce sex to its purely physical components – and that's not in any sense a *meaningful* relationship.

A meaningful relationship, in the eyes of the critics, can take only one prescribed form. But they have to close their eyes to reality to believe that. Your sexual orientation is not some kind of fashion accessory choice. It's inherent. It's visceral, it's elemental, and it affects the direction of your life. The pity of these debates is that people seem unwilling to accept that.

We have many different religious beliefs. We have different sexual orientations. We have different views on morality and the best way to live your life. The whole notion of separating the Church and State was based on the understanding that if you want to maintain some unity between people with differing points of view, you must have a system that allows for tolerance and diversity and plurality. You agree on the bedrock beliefs you all hold in common, you agree on what behaviour is proscribed, and within those parameters, you permit the greatest possible degree of freedom. It's a pretty successful formula, and no matter what any fundamentalist church might argue otherwise, it would seem unwise to relinquish that.

The peculiar thing about morality in New Zealand, Professor

Andrew Sharp notes, is the idea that it's got a lot to do with sex. He says that's very closely connected with the rise of mass politics. Before that, morality would equally have been seen to be about distribution of material goods, about transport, about clean air, for example.

> I would have thought, if you asked me *What's the most serious moral value to New Zealanders?*, it's the way they drive too close on roads or drive fast. These are much more serious threats to human life and welfare than anything to do with sex. But New Zealanders don't so much think of these as being morality issues. We call things moral issues when there's very great disagreement. And the main sign of there being very great disagreement is that none of the political parties can come up with policies on them.

Because political parties can deal with transport and clean air, roads and things, he says, they're called political issues, not moral, and then what's left because there is a disagreement gets called morality. It's trivial stuff – it doesn't really matter. Certainly, issues like this are taken 'very, very seriously by those that believe in them and are committed to them'. But they're not actually serious enough for political parties to bother with.

You might argue that the civil union debate never focused on what could be the real issue: the quality of relationships. How do you ensure that our society is one where those relationships can flourish? We talked about what constitutes an appropriate family in which to raise children, but nothing beyond it. ACT MP Deborah Coddington wishes 'people would get worked up about education standards and the number of children who can't read and write properly rather than civil unions' but, she says, that's the way it is. People who consider the nation's moral fibre to be being eroded are entitled to hold that opinion and 'they're very lucky to be in a country where they can', but it seems to her they're 'just being Chicken Little'.

> The sky's not going to fall in. The same debate was held when the Homosexual Law Reform Bill was going through. And when the Prostitution Bill [came up] last year, there were going to be boatloads of Thai women waiting to come here, set up next to every school; and if anything, it's probably made it harder to set up a brothel because of the local authority by-laws.

She thinks that as we've moved away from religion, something has gone from people's lives: religion is a form of philosophy and no other philosophy has taken its place. People need some form of meaning. She believes in part it's a consequence of removing religious instruction from the schools.

> Well, there's no philosophy at all. I'm not saying replace it with what we call divinity or religious studies, but we should replace it with philosophy. There's no reason why we couldn't have the teachings of all sorts of philosophies from Emmanuel Kant to [Adam] Smith, Sartre, or go through the main ones. *Sophie's World*, [a novel about the history of philosophy by Jostein Gaarder] put it in a very easy to understand way, which was a lovely book as well, but we don't have any of that sort of education. So maybe they'd be less impressionable these youngsters when this charismatic man comes along.

Jeanette Fitzsimons gets 'really, really sick' of people who think that morality is about who you sleep with and has nothing to do with whether your foreign policy causes kids to starve in another country. To them, 'morality has nothing to do with who you invade and how many people you bomb, and corporate-level tax fraud and destruction of the environment. To me, those things are moral issues just as much as the personal behaviour that people seem to target.'

Moral wasteland? Perhaps. But it's an odd wasteland that

passes laws that show more compassion, not less; more tolerance, not less; and more understanding for another person's point of view. You might even call it Christian . . .

Chapter Eleven

HELEN A HAND CART

1 April 2015

Auckland

Recalcitrant commentators Frank Haden and Michael Laws were repatriated from the Tolerance Adjustment Centre on Waiheke Island this morning. In a cordial exchange of views as they made their return to Auckland on the steam ferry, they told the Listener on Sunday *they were glad to be coming home and hoped to see their remaining colleagues repatriated soon. 'Leighton's been there seven years now, and I'm a bit worried he's becoming institutionalised,' Laws confided. He also thought it regrettable that Mike Hosking was still maintaining his hunger strike. 'They only put him in there to stop him going on about wine, but the addiction to publicity was too strong and so he pulled the hunger strike stunt. They say he's the only hunger striker to ever go more than 200 days, but we suspect he's actually sneaking the lentils when no one's looking. They bring an awful lot of the stuff in each week, but none of the rest of us were eating any.' Haden, eyes darting nervously, jokes about looking for a McDonald's outlet where he can get a carton of Rothmans as soon as the ferry reaches Auckland, but acknowledges*

hastily that it's just a joke. 'They'd shut the last one down
long before I went in the first time.' Laws vowed this would
be his only experience of the place. 'The sound of them
flogging Bob Jones each night with a Peruvian tea towel
will haunt me for the rest of my life.'

THE YEAR 2005 got off to an interesting start with the news
that Rugby League hero Graham Lowe was packing his bags and
moving to Australia. Queensland, as it happens. The place was
going to the dogs, and he was off. He was as proud a Kiwi as you
could get, and maybe he was showing his age but he wanted
to remember the New Zealand he grew up in, he said in the *New
Zealand Herald*. 'I don't think it is quite the same at the moment.
I still love the place but the political correctness is just too much
for me.'

Now look what we've done. *Can somebody please stop this
insanity before it ruins us all?* If it's not political correctness that's
undoing us, it's social engineering, and it's all, of course,
emanating from within the forbidding walls of Helengrad.
What can we do about this plague? Actually, I have some
scepticism about all this. I quite like the point of view of writer
Christopher Brookmyre who tagged the expression *It's political
correctness gone mad* as the distress call of the thwarted bigot.

What is it that grieves people? Can we have some examples,
please? Well, one that emerged at the beginning of 2005 was
the outrageous news that police in Auckland had been going
into bars looking for drunk customers.

Wander down to the District Court any morning and
entertain yourself some time. If you can get through the day
without hearing a good deal about alcohol, I'll buy you a double.
The language can be a little emasculated, a little genteel, but
everyone knows what it means. Some eighteen-year-old got

himself loaded and went off his nut. Some married guy was in a bar for six hours and got uglier with every rum and coke until he took to some other guy and gave his head a mashing. Then he went home and wasted his missus.

The police could give you stories like that to last you all day. So if someone somewhere in their Auckland hierarchy decides that it might be worth going into a few bars and looking for any intoxicated customers, what class of *outrage* are we dealing with?

In the simplest terms, it couldn't be more straightforward. The law says you can't serve people who are intoxicated. The police are going into bars to see that the law's being complied with. It's not some new piece of jackbooted nanny-statism just introduced by this administration of crazed social engineers. It was passed in 1989, alongside a pretty substantial liberalisation of the drinking laws. The whole idea was that you'd no longer have a highly regulated regime with closing hours at ten or eleven, and only a limited number of bars per town. And to make sure that this didn't lead to untrammelled debauchery, they also raised the stakes for anyone who was serving the stuff. The bars have never made a secret of this. If you've ever stopped to read the notices they hang all over the place, you'll get the message easily enough: *We won't serve you if you're drunk: we could get fined $10,000.* So into this picture come some Auckland police to see that the bars are complying with the law. Just like they used to do when I was an underage drinker and a sea of blue would wash across the bar as the officers of the team policing unit would establish if we'd correctly memorised the date of birth on the driver's licence we'd borrowed from our older mate.

The charges against the police, according to various disgruntled citizens, are as follows: waste of police time, distortion of priorities, social engineering, and taking it upon themselves to deal with matters that are not their concern. There doesn't seem to be much to warrant a conviction there.

Consider every crime that was committed in the last week. Take the alcohol or the drugs out of the equation, and ask yourself whether as many people would have decided on the spur of the moment – which is how these things quite often take shape – to do it. A police squad moving through bars to ensure that people aren't routinely getting plastered is surely likely to keep bar staff alert to the job. No, it won't stop the ones who are drinking at home, and no, it won't have any relevance to the crimes that the sober ones are committing. But a bar-full of seriously drunk customers is a pretty good recipe for a few assaults and summary offences over the course of a Friday night in the city.

All of this, of course, is as nothing compared to the outrage of the social engineering licensed by this nanny state. Or to put it another way – law enforcement is supposed to be what happens to other people, not middle-class people like me. *If I want to get pissed, or drive fast, that's my right, and how dare they tell me what to do.* Because your rights are mitigated by the rights of others not to be harmed by the consequences of your drinking or your driving perhaps?

To be sure, the senior sergeant who's in charge of policing liquor licence laws for the Auckland City district gave his critics a little ammunition in his defence of the policy by making some remarks about people spending all their money on alcohol. But do we really not want police to be doing some thinking about the causes of crime? He may be right, he may be wrong. But the theory that people might blow all their money on drink and drugs and then become a problem for the rest of us while they wait for more cash doesn't sound entirely implausible. You might address that with social policy, you might address it with some police activity. And maybe you might address it with a blend of the two. It's a fair topic for debate though, surely, and it seems reflexive to say simply that this is no business of the police.

Social engineering is what, exactly? Teaching our children? Censorship? Recognising people in the New Year Honours? The State gets involved in making and expressing all kinds of judgements and encouraging or coercing people to behave in certain ways, and it was doing it long before this administration took office.

It's also worth bearing in mind just how much of the so-called social engineering we see here is really just an implementation of comparable measures being used by various other Western democracies. Smoking, for example. Drugs. Sexual health. Addiction treatment. Mental illness. Crime. Workplace safety. Road safety. Things, in short, that harm you, and quite possibly kill you. For some odd reason, these are issues that exercise many nations. Bureaucrats and academics study these matters, make recommendations, experiment with solutions and then unleash them on unwitting citizens. The further you move into prevention and the best means of cure, the further you risk incursions on individual rights. Smoke-free environments, for example. Oh, the gnashing of nicotine-stained teeth we got over that.

Russell Brown notes that although people complained that this was social engineering, every single poll showed the same response. 'When they're polled, people say it's actually quite a good idea.' Oddly enough, he says, the actual results of opinion polls don't always seem to come into play when people are pronouncing on the issue. 'People speak as if they're coming from a majority viewpoint, and you saw that with the civil union thing, and there was simply no proof that that was the case. But maybe their argument would be hard to sustain if they actually accepted that they were coming from a minority viewpoint.'

Could it be that social engineering is really just a phrase people use to describe democracy they don't like? Russell Brown suspects it could be, and he also thinks that social engineering, like political correctness, means whatever you want it to mean. He recalls in 2004 interviewing Murray McCully on radio, and listening to him 'rave on about something being political correctness gone mad.' Brown stopped and asked:

> Should we perhaps, just before we go any further, define political correctness in this context? Can you define it for me? And he said, No, not really. Then he paused and said: It's not easy. And I found that extraordinary, that there was this thing that was supposedly overtaking us and poisoning the heart of our society and we didn't know what the bloody thing looked like.

Let's try Muriel Newman, then. She emerged, guns blazing, at the beginning of the 2005 election year with a campaign against political correctness and a website to boot: www.pcfreenz.co.nz, which opens with the rallying cry End Political Correctness, for which weapon number one appears to be a petition to get smoking back into 'licenced clubs, such as RSAs and sports clubs, and to licenced premises where all employees give written consent to permit smoking.'

And she's dog on Lowey shooting through. 'It is indeed a sad day for New Zealand when political correctness has infiltrated our society to the level where it is driving good Kiwis abroad. Left alone, its proliferation does not bode well for the future of our society,' she lamented in a newsletter a week or two after the shock announcement.

McCully might not have had the words at his disposal, but

Muriel harbours no illusions, and she waves the red flag. 'Political correctness is an ideology that originated in the former Soviet Union during the early 1900s. The Marxists realised that the secret to controlling the way citizens think is to control their language. To progress this ideology they adopted the official rationale that they were restricting the use of 'hurtful' expressions in order to prevent offence.'

And it's run amok. The proponents of political correctness use intimidation and criticism as weapons to muzzle free speech and frank expression. 'Hate labels such as racist, sexist, homophobe or redneck are widely used to describe those who speak out against politically correct initiatives. The use of vicious, personal attack is intended to silence the opposition.'

It wasn't always like this, she points out. It started out as a bit of a laugh. We were discouraged from using words like mankind or chairman, and buying golliwogs or repeating blonde jokes was frowned upon. 'But now, it has all gone too far.'

She rolls out the sinister matter of her district council, which is proposing name-changes to the local mountain and river. Officially she says, the move is to 'correct' historical spelling mistakes, but she taps her nose knowingly. 'Locals have labelled the proposals as political correctness gone mad.'

But now we have to do a little contorting. Although these evil social engineers are changing names against our will, it turns out they're doing it though a shadowy process known as 'public consultation' and, she helpfully explains, concerned locals are being encouraged to make submissions. It is only, she says, by speaking out and standing up against the PC onslaught that its relentless progression can be stopped:

> Everyone in New Zealand should be free to express their views as they see fit. While we may not necessarily agree with their views, we should vigorously defend their right to state them

without fear or favour. That freedom of speech is at the heart of our democracy. It is central to 'the Kiwi way'. Retaining our proud straight-talking tradition is surely worth fighting for.

Well, er, yes. And isn't that just the point? No, it's not ever acceptable to chill public debate by intimidation, and there was any amount of that going on behind the Iron Curtain (and let's not forget the diligent efforts of Senator McCarthy and friends either). But isn't it a bit of a stretch to assert that the practice of using 'hate labels such as racist, sexist, homophobe or redneck' amounts to a chilling intimidation? You say intimidation, I say debate. If there's no substance to the label, it's easily enough dismissed.

Not that there haven't been moments. There was a period, Russell Brown thinks, in the early 1980s, where 'we got a little touch of that thing that swept the universities in particular, where people were too scared to speak'. He recalls that there were men who resolved to become gay 'so they wouldn't be oppressing women':

> There was a guy that we lived with in this big flat who somehow managed to parlay that *not oppressing women* into getting up a threesome with his partner and another politically sound gay woman. It was extraordinary. Apparently it wasn't oppression if you were outnumbered!
>
> But you know, that's not exaggeration, that happened. There *were* people – a limited number, no doubt – who thought that. We certainly have swung back from those excesses. I knew girls back then who felt intimidated for wearing *make-up* at university. That was ludicrous. And I do find it odd that we hear so much now that it's a problem, when on the basis of observation, we appear to be on a rather more sensible tack now.

If you were accusing the Labour Government of social engineering, you might pick the civil union legislation, the prostitution reform, the smoking – what else might irk people?:

Often they're quite minor things. In the – I think – Care of Children Bill – there were a few things that people really objected to, including the redefining of 'father'. They decided that a lesbian parent would have to be denoted – purely as an administrative convenience – as a father; and of course it was, *Oh, here we go, we've got women being fathers, it's political correctness gone mad*. And it was a convenience for administration, it was the easiest way of dealing with it.

I thought that the civil union issue just should never have been as controversial as it was, when you think that it was actually in the manifesto that Labour went into the last election with. It had been talked about for at least three years before that, and there just hadn't been any kind of panic about it, and then I think those sorts of churches had reached a certain degree of momentum and you had the Maxim Institute there. I think you've seen people lend their names to Maxim in part because it looks to them as though these people are terribly scientific and it looks as though they know what they're doing, and it also looks as though they have broad-based support whereas most of Maxim's money continues to come from [Auckland Textile Business] Derek Corporation. There are not tens of thousands of people giving money to them.

People, both from the left *and* the right have this belief that we had some golden age in New Zealand, Brown says. 'And it wasn't so. Okay, there were times when we were certainly on the pig's back *economically*, but the more and more we've become an open society, the more we discover what we covered up back then – domestic violence was one thing, but look at the Waiouru cadet school thing. How many years did that go on? There were *rapes*.'

He's certain we are a much more open society than we were. 'And that sort of leads on to this idea that we *are* going to hell in a handcart and it's all terrible and all these social indicators are in freefall, which I actually had put to me.' He recalls interviewing Bruce Logan of the Maxim Institute, who had argued that social indicators were in freefall – divorce and child abuse, for example. But: 'I went to look at it and it simply wasn't true. The divorce one is really interesting, because the divorce rate having trended steadily upwards for fifteen years to 1980 when the law was transferred to the Family Court and changed to make it less onerous – as you might expect, it spiked for the next two years, came down quite sharply and has plateaued ever since.' There's a reasonable case, presumably, for saying that if the law hadn't been amended and that the trend that had been demonstrated up to 1980 had continued, the divorce rate would have been much higher than it is now. Our divorce rate is much lower than, for example, America's, but what about de facto relationships where relationships constitute and reconstitute? What about young parents not forming a lasting relationship and typically moving on to other ones?

> Or where there are situations where the relationship might stay together for the early years of the child's life and then perhaps drift apart. Yeah, I think that happens. But the research shows that couples who cohabit before marrying have a higher divorce rate than those who don't, but the difference disappears after eight years of marriage. It's certainly become more socially acceptable to be a solo mother and more viable, but it's not as if the DPB is spinning out of control.

You also, Brown thinks, have to balance that against the fact that whilst a lot of men in the '60s and '70s might have *technically* been married, the responsibility they assumed for actually caring for their children was often minimal, 'whereas now it's an absolute given that you get involved, you're at the birth, you change the nappies and you give emotional as well as financial support, and I think that's a beneficial change'.

> And that brings you on to the whole thing of domestic violence, where it was barely considered an offence; the police had very

little power to act on it, and that's changed.

Then we get on to the perception of a crime wave. We had the Christchurch *Press* saying: *Crime continues inexorably to rise after a decade of economic prosperity.* Well, no, it doesn't! I thought it was absolutely extraordinary that a major newspaper could make that claim in its editorial page – a fine proposition apart from the facts.

And when you're talking about moral crimes – sexual offending in a climate where you would expect the likelihood of reporting to have vastly increased, reported sexual offences have been trending slowly downwards. It's been pretty flat since 1994, but it's falling and we've got a far lower incidence of sex crime than say Australia. We've actually done really well, which tends to militate against this idea that we've got moral turpitude – you know, the moral abyss thing. Actually, we're going quite well.

But of course if people see, of six news items, two or three regarding crime, they're going to remain convinced that we're in the grip of a wave aren't they? Yes, Brown agrees, there's a demonstrated trend of coverage of crime in the papers.

As crime fell, from the early 1990s, the coverage of crime in the media increased. And it was the more serious, more alarming crimes that make up the smallest proportion – the coverage of those increased more. And people, when they have been questioned, have consistently overestimated the incidence and the severity of crime. And consistently underestimated the sentences that are handed out. Because the sentences have gone up as well, whereas people had this perception – because that was what they'd been told by the media, who were reporting politicians – that we've gone soft. Whereas if you look at it through the nineties, actual sentences for any given offence in most cases went up.

It's all the fault of the media, then? Perhaps not, but there does seem to be a thread that runs through so much of our shared culture that puts undue emphasis on the exception, rather than the rule. A visitor from outer space might get the impression from absorbing twenty-four hours of our media that the world is composed of celebrities, criminals, business moguls, sports stars, movie stars, and perhaps a software genius or two. Twenty-four hours of our local media would probably give them the sense that when they're not trying to impose thought control on its citizens, the nation's bureaucrats are shamelessly wasting money on earnestly worthy yet utterly frivolous pursuits, from hip hop studies to degree courses in golf.

The boring truth of the matter is that most people lead less spectacular lives, earn less money and enjoy less prestige than the objects of media fascination. Meanwhile, the nation's bureaucrats for the most part administer the tens of billions of annual expenditure in New Zealand, allocating it in the greatest proportion to the equally unspectacular business of running such entities as hospitals, schools and police stations in spectacularly routine and conventional ways. But there's no headline in that, and less scope for the disgruntled critic to pin the government's ears to the wall over egregious social engineering and PC madness. The exception, when it's found, is seized upon and brandished for the smoking gun it never was.

None of which is to say that either the government or the progressive left is beyond reproach. Errors of judgement are made. Woolly bleeding-heart notions get their outings. Ill-considered programmes of the worthiest and most earnest stripe make their shaky way into the light of day.

Worse, the left can be very hypocritical about practising the tolerance it espouses. And this administration seems to have the knack of undermining perfectly sound ideas by packaging them in a form of wowserish finger-wagging. It was perhaps not surprising that 'bossy government' should have made it into the list of concerns expressed by participants in a *Herald* poll at the beginning of 2005, even if it was just 1.5 per cent of them.

For all that, though, these seem to be more considerate, more tolerant times. The New Zealand I grew up in is the same one Lowey remembers. It was a dull, intolerant, conformist society, run by middle-aged white men for middle-aged white men. I'm sorry he misses it. I prefer the one we have now. Blogger NoRightTurn responded to a series of articles in the *Dominion Post* in 2004 which had asked: *Are we in a moral wasteland?* by posting an assessment of the changed times.

In the New Zealand of 1971, he reminded us:

- it wasn't just legal to pay a woman less than a man for the same work – it was mandatory under most national awards;

- it was legal for shopkeepers to refuse to serve Maori or Catholics – and many did;

- beating your wife and kids was socially acceptable, and police would simply walk away from a 'domestic';

- there was 'spousal immunity' for rape;

- homosexuality wasn't just illegal; juries would refuse to convict those who murdered gays.

Today, he said, we don't allow discrimination, we protect women and children from abuse, 'no' *means* 'no', and the State does not care what happens in the bedrooms of consenting adults. He also wrote, in a related context:

> Look at who complains about 'political correctness'. Look at what they are complaining about. If we take those complaints at face value, then 'political correctness' stands for the expansion of equality and opportunity and the erosion of entrenched privilege. And that is something we need more of, not less.

He liked the notion that we had become more tolerant and inclusive. So do I. If that's a slide into the abyss, let's keep right on going.

HAVE YOUR SAY

A betting market can be a kind of continuous popular referendum. So what would happen if you had a betting market on aspects of New Zealand's future? Why not open one and find out? This book has a companion website which offers you the chance to place your bets on where we're going.

Go to www.optimisticpredictions.com and you will get an imaginary $100 to wager on each of the fifteen predictions about New Zealand's future. As soon as you place your bet, the market is updated, and the new odds are displayed.

The market offers six predictions based upon this section of the book:

- PC-obsessed government outlaws dissent; nationalises all media.

- Gay-friendly policies lead one in three males to change sexual orientation.

- Destiny Church numbers exceed 200,000.

- Last New Zealand nuclear family splits up.

To place your bet, go to www.optimisticpredictions.com

Conclusion

IF THIS story isn't true, it ought to be. Apparently there is a shop somewhere in England with this sign in its window:

> We have been established for over one hundred years and have been pleasing or displeasing customers ever since. We have made money and lost money, suffered the effects of coal nationalisation, coal rationing, government control, and bad payers. We have been cussed and discussed, messed about, lied to, held up, robbed, and swindled. The only reason we stay in business is to see what happens next.

One of the things I like about the New Zealand attitude is that we're quite likely to laugh at bad luck. Perhaps we have the view that it's been a bit of a roll of the dice trying to make a go of a country at the bottom of the world, thousands of miles from anywhere. We've come unstuck often enough, but by any measure, you'd have to say that the roll of the dice has actually paid off. There are more than four million of us generating more than 100 billion dollars' worth of GDP a year. We were, for a little while, one of the richest nations on the planet. If you were an adult at that time, though, you probably didn't take too much assurance from that. My parents' generation grew up in the shadow of the Depression, and it seems to me they'll never forget what that meant. They also lived through world war. They remain, it seems to me, a little on guard against calamity.

By comparison, the half-century that I've lived through has

been remarkably benign by any historical standard. No pandemic, no world war, rising prosperity, no depression. The optimists say it will stay that way. ACT party president Catherine Judd, at their 2005 conference, recommended the proposition by Matthew Parris in *The Spectator* that 'we should be glorying in the fact that the right has won the argument'. They were, she said, 'part of modernity, part of the winning side of the argument'. (The actual comment by Parris was: 'The Right has won the argument, so why is it so angry and sour?' *The Spectator*, 20 November 2004) Supporters of individual freedom should be able to grin.

Well, maybe. As the saying goes about the French Revolution and its impact: it could be too soon to tell. The more-market economic orthodoxy holds all the cards for now, to be sure. But to hold, it needs to ensure the cohesion of those societies. Maybe the ubiquity of consumerism and the aspirations it creates among its poorest will be sufficient. But a society short on spiritual fulfilment does seem to go looking for it. And the answers people find may or may not keep them dutifully turning the wheels in their little hamster cages.

Tim Hazledine told me: 'I wouldn't want to be born now basically, I must say. There are some really big issues in the world, mainly sustainability issues, I think, that we're not recognising at the moment.' But, he said, 'I like to think I'm an optimistic sort of person and perhaps we'll come to grips with it – sooner rather than later would be better.'

Who to believe? The ideal from this point on sees prosperity and democracy spreading out across the globe, and all boats rising. Who wouldn't hope for that? But history so far suggests that you don't tend to get smooth sailing for too very long. Some of those factors are entirely beyond our control. Tsunamis, earthquakes and cyclones all prove that. Some are arguably within our control: pandemic, environmental catastrophe. If you want something to truly worry about, worry about them. Worry, but also hope that we manage to use our ever-wider accumulated knowledge to meet the challenge.

For most of humanity, the notion of Hobbes' assessment of a solitary, poor, nasty, brutish existence was discouragingly accurate. Enormous catastrophe could perhaps put us back into such a position. But would that be the end? Any number of generations before us had to deal with that: seeking, over-coming odds, and hanging on by an altogether thinner thread.

If you tallied up all the dreadful ways the world could end tomorrow, you'd never get out of bed. Volcano, meteor, trans-mutating virus, nuclear catastrophe – it's horrible. But we do get up, and we whistle each day past the graveyard. By contrast, much of what we fret about here in New Zealand – as others quite probably do to an equivalent extent in other places – looks like small beer: Treaty arguments, morality arguments, PC and social engineering arguments, scraps over the way we run the economy. That's not to say they don't merit debate, but it pays to keep a sense of proportion about them.

So with that sense of proportion in mind, what can we say about them? The economy? New Zealand might not be the lucky country, but how about 'plucky'? We're able to be adaptable, agile and adventurous. We've tried new things, we've pioneered things, and we like the notion of doing it. We get interesting results. We're in a good position to do more of that, if we were of a mind. That would count for plenty in managing, as Rod Oram proposes, to *thrive*, rather than *survive*. We are, to be sure, hooked into a world network that exerts strong influences in culture, in trading markets, in finance, for example, and we get pushed and pulled by that. But our size, our stability and our relative prosperity means we're better able to experiment with things than many countries. Why be timid? Why not make the most of that?

We hear about the way business is strangled by compliance costs here, but I wouldn't be so sure about that – in the land of the free and the home of the brave, things can be pretty demanding. Ask anyone who's worked on a listing on the New York Stock Exchange. A lawyer friend of mine maintains that this remains one of the most straightforward places to set up a business. I liked a title comedian Mike King once said he was going to be using for a TV show he had coming up. Either it didn't see the light of day or he changed it, but I liked the one he started with: *At least you're having a go, son.* I've always liked the expression, because although it's a not-so-subtle putdown, it captures something about the way things work here. People do have a go, even if they're hopelessly out of their depth.

Michael Cullen made a speech not so long ago discouraging people from cherishing the myth of the clever Kiwi inventor in his shed. The point he was making was a fair one – that you can actually manage your development in a more systematic and controlled way – and I'm not sure he was saying there wasn't a place for the inventor within that environment. But I know just from my own experience that although you can come up with a clever idea and turn it into a foreign exchange-earning money-spinner, you're not doing the thing justice if you do it all as a one-man band. We need, as Rod Oram points out, to get better at building up to the big-scale stuff. But is it doable? I don't think there's much doubt about that.

As to our other great dilemmas, I think the most telling point about this business of civil war is that all through our history, in the various confrontations, the guns kept missing. I think they will keep missing here, because we all have too much to lose. For similar reasons I think we'll manage to wade our way through the moral and ethical morass that causes so much anxiety for so many. We're an adolescent society, getting accustomed to the notion that you can have different people with different points of view, and that it's possible for a sophisticated nation to accommodate a true plurality of views.

We seem to have a race debate in this country every couple of years. A few years ago it was Asian immigration. A few years before that it was Pacific Island workers. There's always going to be someone who comes along and tries to make cheap political capital out of piling into some racial group in New Zealand. But you can't make long-term political capital by being someone who takes one group of New Zealanders and sets them apart from the others, because in the end, I think, we're decent and we have a sense of fairness.

But I can't say any of this with certainty. Just as you can write books predicting the future, you can also write books compiling a wide variety of woefully inaccurate predictions; Christopher Cerf and Victor Navasky did in *The Experts Speak* – a compendium of authoritative predictions made in the past which turned out to be wonderfully wrong, usually almost immediately. For example: Irving Fisher, professor of economics at Yale University, said, on 17 October 1929, that *Stocks have reached what looks like a permanently high plateau.* Lord Kelvin said in 1897 that *Radio has no future.* And Bill Clinton would lose to *any Republican who doesn't drool on stage*, according to *The Wall Street Journal* in 1995.

We can learn, then, from history. What's old is often new, and it seems somehow apposite to mention an observation Sir Tipene O'Regan made when I interviewed him for *Bullshit, Backlash & Bleeding Hearts*. He was talking about having to sit round reading 'bloody Morgan' (economist and columnist Gareth Morgan in the *Sunday Star-Times*) sounding off about 'the Maori collective' when every company that he dispensed share advice about was a 'Pakeha collective'.

> I take him back to the Hon. Mr Rees. It's about 1879. It's an appendix to the Journals of the House of Representatives. A memorandum – he's getting really uptight about attempts to destroy Maori collective rights and interests. Anyway, Mr Rees observes and opines: it is an extraordinary thing that we, who have spent 400 years developing the concept of the limited liability company, should come to this remote and distant place and here find this structure in its most near-perfect form, and immediately set about its destruction.

I like that. This is a place where you will find smart thinking, and you won't always find it where you might initially think to look. That's how a successful gamble sometimes goes. You don't always follow the conventional wisdom or even the smart money, and sometimes your horse can come storming home from the back and upset them all. You can live on a result like that for years.

Bibliography

lves, Dora, *The Maori and the Crown*. Greenwood Press, 1999.

Belgrave, Michael; Kawharu, Merata; Williams, David, *Waitangi Revisited – Perspectives on the Treaty of Waitangi*. Oxford University Press, 2004.

Brookfield, F.M. (Jock), *Waitangi & Indigenous Rights: Revolution, Law and Legitimation*. Auckland University Press, 1999.

Consedine, Robert and Consedine, Joanna, *Healing our History – The Challenge of the Treaty of Waitangi*. Penguin, 2001.

Coates, Ken S. and McHugh, P.G., *Living Relationships: Kokiri Ngatahi – The Treaty of Waitangi in the New Millennium*. Victoria University Press, 1998.

Diamond, Paul, *A Fire in Your Belly*. Huia, 2003.

Gould, Stephen Jay, *Rocks of Ages – Science and Religion in the Fullness of Life*. Vintage, 2001.

Hill, Michael; Mast, Sharon; Bowman, Richard; Carr-Gregg, Charlotte, *Shades of Deviance*. Dunmore Press, 1983.

King, Michael, *Being Pakeha Now*. Penguin, 1999.

Lomborg, Bjorn, *The Real State of the World*. New Zealand Business Roundtable, 2003.

Minogue, Kenneth, *Waitangi, Morality and Reality*. New Zealand Business Roundtable, 1998.

Orange, Claudia, *An Illustrated History of The Treaty of Waitangi*. Bridget Williams Books, 2004.

Sharp, Andrew, *Justice and the Maori*. Oxford University Press, 1990.

Sharp, Andrew and Paul McHugh, *Histories, Power and Loss*. Bridget Williams Books, 2001.

Shorto, Russell, *The Island at the Centre of the World*. Doubleday, 2004.

Walker, Ranginui, *Ka Whawhai Tonu Matou: Struggle Without End*. Penguin, 2004.

Bullshit, Backlash & Bleeding Hearts

David Slack

The best-selling book that digs behind the slogans, myths, mud-slinging and misconceptions on ALL sides of the current Treaty and race debate to explain exactly where we are, how we got here and where we're heading.

'A brisk, cheerful crash-course in local history'
Margo White, *Metro*

'This is the book the public needs for answers to current thorny Treaty questions'
Claudia Orange, author of *The Treaty of Waitangi*